"The interactive presence of God pu_____ Like Me? and into our daily lives. A vibrant and relau.... all of Scripture and now engages our personal lives. Through the exercises in each chapter, we learn to interact with Jesus in ways that transform who we are and how we live. Maybe you have believed or maybe you are not sure if God really works—it is time to try God's living presence for yourself."

Jim Wilder, neurotheologian and theoretician at Life Model Works (formerly Shepherd's House), author and international speaker on relational Christianity, trauma recovery, and character development in community

"Through engaging stories, lived wisdom, formative practices, and incisive reflection questions, Geoff and Cyd Holsclaw carefully and compassionately offer answers to many of the significant questions we ask of God, others, and ourselves. This book will help you see many deeply held and inaccurate cultural perceptions about God and replace them with the truth about who he really is—the one who sees, knows, and delights in those he has created. If you know in your head that God loves you, but you wrestle in your heart and soul with whether God actually *likes* you, I'm confident this resource will help you to catch a glimpse of the smiling face of your loving heavenly Father."

J. R. Briggs, founder of Kairos Partnerships, author of *Fail: Finding Hope and Grace in the Midst of Ministry Failure*

"The Bible is adamant that God loves us; most Christians know this. But many have a difficult time embracing the idea that God not only loves them, he likes them too. They fail to realize that this is, in fact, the heart of the gospel: that God so loved the world that he gave his son—in the most generous and intimate way imaginable—in order to restore us to a friendship with him. As wise and competent tour guides, Cyd and Geoff Holsclaw take us on a journey through Scripture to help us rediscover the vital and liberating truth that God delights in us, takes joy in our presence, and wants to be with us forever."

Andrew Arndt, teaching pastor at New Life Church, Colorado Springs, Colorado

"Written with honesty and grace, *Does God Really Like Me?* makes the case that God indeed likes us and longs to be with us. In a world dominated by feelings of deficiency, distress, and dislike, we badly need to hear the message of this book and to live into it: God loves me, and God likes me, and by God's grace, so can I."

James Bryan Smith, author of *The Good and Beautiful God*

"A. W. Tozer famously quipped, 'What comes into our minds when we think about God is the most important thing about us.' Cyd and Geoff Holsclaw dig deeper into this reality, going beyond thinking and cognition to the everyday, relational presence of the triune God. *Does God Really Like Me?* is an integrative look at how we actually experience God in our lives, weaving insights from biblical theology, neuroscience, and decades of Cyd and Geoff's pastoral wisdom. This treatment is a gift to the church; it immediately goes at the top of the list as an additional resource for those in the Gravity Leadership Academy. Our training of leaders to walk with Jesus, experience his love, and abide in his presence moment by moment benefits greatly by this accessible and profound book."

Matt Tebbe, cofounder of Gravity Leadership, copastor at The Table in Indianapolis

"It can seem today as if most people are big God-denying sinners! But I think something else lies under this observation: most people are sensitive souls seeking practical confidence in God via heartfelt questions—Am I truly welcome anywhere in life? If I am accurately seen, will I be exposed? Can I ever feel at home in this chaotic, fleeting world? Does anyone see me, know me, or care about me? As a decades-long follower of Jesus and as a pastor I have both had these thoughts and heard them from thousands of others. In *Does God Really Like Me?* by Geoff Holsclaw and Cyd Holsclaw, you will discover their experience-based and thoughtful grasp on this challenge—and their ability to guide us past our most gut-wrenching inner questions to the always-ready, always-there love of God."

Todd Hunter, bishop of the Anglican Diocese of Churches for the Sake of Others

"Geoff and Cyd Holsclaw have given the church and the seeker a gift with their first book together. Their vision of the grand narrative of the Bible, personal vulnerability, and invitations to application and reflection present the reader with multiple avenues for receiving their important message. God's invitation to intimacy and deep desire to dwell with humankind is presented with accessible breadth and depth. They cover the major epochs of God's reconciling mission and present the Cross as the ultimate expression of God's pursuing love for the lost. I commend this book for all believers, especially those wrestling with deep feelings of inadequacy or in recovery from profound moments of rejection. May God use these insights and stories for the healing and liberation of many."

Charlie Self, professor of church history at Assemblies of God Theological Seminary, director of learning communities for the Made to Flourish network

"If this faith is supposed to be about love, why does it so often feel like dry obligation? Perhaps it's our capacity to even receive his love that God wants to heal. To do so he uses people like the Holsclaws. Through Scripture, story, imagery, and even music, they invite us to immerse into the possibility that this faith can be emotionally satisfying, that we can truly belong and be known by God."

Mandy Smith, pastor of University Christian Church, Cincinnati, Ohio, and author of *The Vulnerable Pastor*

"Geoff and Cyd Holsclaw have a gift for communicating the joy of the gospel in practical and life-giving ways. Through their comprehensive and perceptive exploration of Scripture, they demonstrate that the good news is so much better than what we often live or even imagine. If you've ever struggled to fully embrace the truth that God loves you *and* delights in you, *Does God Really Like Me?* is a reorienting and reassuring read."

Sharon Garlough Brown, author of the Sensible Shoes Series and *Shades of Light*

"With the wisdom of pastors and the depth of theologians, Cyd and Geoff Holsclaw write *Does God Really Like Me?* Its winsome prose and wonderful stories will draw you into the world made known in Jesus Christ, where God is so 'glad to be with us.' And so I welcome you, without reservation, to read this book and discover a path out of dryness with God. A profoundly deep, faithful, and biblical masterpiece for our times."

David Fitch, B. R. Lindner Chair of Evangelical Theology at Northern Seminary Chicago, author of *Faithful Presence*

"If you've ever wondered if there is anything really good or likable in the good news of the Christian story—about who you are, or who God is, or about life with God—then listen to it again with Cyd and Geoff Holsclaw. And begin to practice with them this gift of life and love and liked-ness. They know our God and our family story, and they help us see the biblical pattern of God's unstoppable life and love for and with us, of his delight in and purposes for us, woven with the unbreakable beauty of divine joy. Settle in, get (un)comfortable, and begin the renewal that comes with hearing, seeing, and experiencing God's joy over you as his beloved, image-bearing child in his permanent family. Listen well. The Holsclaws tell their story of homecoming and reshaping through discovering what it means to be loved and liked by (thus becoming like) God, who has woven his own joy-filled life and Spirit into the flesh and fabric of our lives forever in Jesus. Try it. You'll like being liked by God. Just ask Geoff and Cyd."

Cherith Fee Nordling, author of *Knowing God by Name*

"We absolutely must recover from a shame-based theology. You and I are meant to live from our identity as God's image bearers—shame be damned! Geoff and Cyd Holsclaw offer a winsome road map helping us orient toward the reality of God's love for us, out of our shame and into the presence and story of God. God in fact likes us very much—we belong to him and he is always glad to be with us. The Holsclaws bring us the depth of a theological anthropology from creation to consummation—served up with stories and metaphors from their own lives—inviting us toward a clearer understanding of how God sees us."

Jared Patrick Boyd, pastor, spiritual director, and author of *Imaginative Prayer: A Yearlong Guide to Your Child's Spiritual Formation*

Does God Really Like Me?

*Discovering the God
Who Wants to Be With Us*

Cyd Holsclaw *and* Geoff Holsclaw

An imprint of InterVarsity Press
Downers Grove, Illinois

InterVarsity Press
P.O. Box 1400, Downers Grove, IL 60515-1426
ivpress.com
email@ivpress.com

InterVarsity Press® is the book-publishing division of InterVarsity Christian Fellowship/USA®, a movement of students and faculty active on campus at hundreds of universities, colleges, and schools of nursing in the United States of America, and a member movement of the International Fellowship of Evangelical Students. For information about local and regional activities, visit intervarsity.org.

Scripture quotations, unless otherwise noted, are from the New Revised Standard Version of the Bible, copyright 1989 by the Division of Christian Education of the National Council of the Churches of Christ in the USA. Used by permission. All rights reserved.

While any stories in this book are true, some names and identifying information may have been changed to protect the privacy of individuals.

Cover design and image composite: Chris Tobias
Interior design: Daniel van Loon
Image: © Renata Ramsini / Arcangel Images

ISBN 978-0-8308-4596-5 (print)
ISBN 978-0-8308-4822-5 (digital)

Printed in the United States of America ∞

InterVarsity Press is committed to ecological stewardship and to the conservation of natural resources in all our operations. This book was printed using sustainably sourced paper.

Library of Congress Cataloging-in-Publication Data
Names: Holsclaw, Cyd, 1972- author. | Holsclaw, Geoff, author.
Title: Does God really like me? : discovering the God who wants to be with us / Cyd Holsclaw and Geoff Holsclaw.
Description: Downers Grove, IL : IVP, an imprint of InterVarsity Press, 2020. | Includes bibliographical references.
Identifiers: LCCN 2019042902 (print) | LCCN 2019042903 (ebook) | ISBN 9780830845965 (print) | ISBN 9780830848225 (digital)
Subjects: LCSH: Spirituality—Christianity. | God (Christianity)—Love.
Classification: LCC BV4501.3 .H667 2020 (print) | LCC BV4501.3 (ebook) | DDC 248.4—dc23
LC record available at https://lccn.loc.gov/2019042902
LC ebook record available at https://lccn.loc.gov/2019042903

P 25 24 23 22 21 20 19 18 17 16 15 14 13 12 11 10 9 8 7 6 5 4 3 2 1

Y 37 36 35 34 33 32 31 30 29 28 27 26 25 24 23 22 21 20

To Soren and Tennyson. May you always be confident of

your belonging to God and be courageous in offering

your unique blessing to the world.

Contents

Introduction

I don't know what I did wrong. But he had that "calmer than calm" look that hid a rage inside.

I picked up the phone and saw her name. Not now. I can't handle her right now.

I scanned the room, looking for someone I knew. I just wanted to disappear. I didn't have the energy for small talk. So I got more appetizers.

"How dare you!" he screamed. Then he let loose about everything that's wrong with me.

If I said anything, she would just blow up again. So I let it go.

We've all experienced situations like these. We've felt disconnected and judged, overwhelmed by friends and underwhelmed by our relatives. We know how it feels when someone doesn't want us around. And we know how it feels when someone is sucking up all our energy. We've been yelled at. And we've yelled back. We've been ignored. We've done the ignoring. We've felt people were just putting up with us. And we've just put up with others too.

Whether we know it or not, all these experiences color our experience of God. If you've been ignored, scolded, or shamed, then you've probably wondered—consciously or unconsciously—if God is ignoring, scolding, or shaming you. Or, more painfully, maybe you think God is just putting up with you.

We're told that God loves us. But the real question is, Does God really like me?

God Has To . . .

Parents sometimes say that while they certainly love their children, they don't always like them. We get it. We both love our children with a fierce and uncompromising love. We would never abandon them or hurt them. But there have been times when it's hard to like them.

Sometimes it's because of what is going on with us, and sometimes it's what's going on with them. Sometimes the best we can do is just tolerate our loved ones until it gets better—putting up with them because we have to.

And we've all been on the receiving end of this experience too. A parent or some other loved one tells us they love us when they clearly don't like us very much at that moment—and maybe they would rather not be with us either. We get the real message loud and clear.

After enough of these experiences it's easy to believe God feels the same way about us. God promises to love us. But we actually come to believe that God is just putting up with us, tolerating us because he has to, not because he wants to.

God has to love me, we think, *but God doesn't like me*.

But What If?

What if God really does like you?

What if God is always glad to be with you?

What if God is filled with joy because of you?

What if God is always moving toward you and not just keeping his distance? What if God likes you so much that he truly enjoys being with you? What if God appreciates you so much that he wants to partner with you to accomplish all his purposes in the world?

You might be skeptical. Maybe you think all this sounds cheesy or naive. Maybe it's even offensive or disgraceful to think the God of the universe likes you and wants to be with you. Maybe it doesn't line up with your understanding of God's sovereignty or majesty. Maybe it makes God sound pathetic or needy or all too human.

But here's the thing: We've become convinced—through studying the Bible, through meeting God personally in prayer, and through living with God in community with others—that it's all true.

We're convinced that everything changes when we believe God is glad to be with us. It changes how we experience God's presence. It changes how we live. It will change your life. When we trust that God wants to be with us, we learn to live as if we belong with God, as if we're really wanted by God. When we trust that God is giving purpose to our lives, we can freely offer our lives as a blessing to others.

An Appetizer

Here is a small taste of what it means that God longs to be *with us* and to work *through us*. It's a little appetizer before the main course in the chapters ahead. It comes from the Gospel of Matthew.

The Gospel of Matthew is bookended by two stories. The first is the angel's visit to Joseph. After finding out that his bride-to-be was already pregnant, Joseph planned to break off his engagement with Mary. But an angel intervenes to reassure Joseph that Mary's pregnancy is all part of God's plan. Then, like a narrative voice-over in a movie, Matthew explains to his readers that Mary's pregnancy is a fulfillment of Isaiah's prophecy that a virgin would bear a son whose name would be Immanuel. And just so we don't miss it, Matthew tells us what that name means: "God is with us" (Matthew 1:21-23).

This might seem like an insignificant detail at the beginning of the book. But let's go to the end of Matthew's Gospel. The last chapter ends with what is often called the Great Commission. Jesus sends his followers to all nations to make disciples, baptizing and teaching them all the ways of Jesus.

But notice the last thing Jesus says to his disciples. Wherever his disciples go, whatever they might face, Jesus tells them, "Remember, I am with you always" (Matthew 28:20).

I am with you always!

These are the last words in Matthew's Gospel. It's no coincidence that Matthew begins by describing the birth of Jesus as Immanuel, "God with us," and ends with Jesus announcing, "I am with you always."

Matthew is making crystal clear that the main course in the meal of salvation is *God with us*. And *God with us* is not just something that happened in the past. It's a continual and permanent promise reaching into the present moment of our lives. God promises to be with us. Always. No matter what.

In fact, we're going to see that God dwelling with us is *the main point* of the entire biblical story. Not just from the beginning to the end of Matthew's Gospel but from the beginning in Genesis to the end in Revelation. God longs to dwell with humanity. And only from this place of God *with us* is God also working *through us.*

But this is just an appetizer. And you can't live off appetizers. We need a full meal. To get this full meal—to receive God's daily bread—we need to know and experience God differently, and we need to read and understand the Bible differently.

When the (Biblical) Meal Falls Short

Have you ever walked into your local grocery store and found that everything has been moved? You go to the produce section only to find bulk nuts and seeds. You go to the cereal aisle and find paper goods instead. It might take twice as long to get everything on your list because nothing is where it used to be. It's all the same stuff, but it's not where you expect to find it.

We think eggs belong in the dairy section because that's where they have always been. But eggs really have nothing to do with cows or milk! Eggs and milk are both good things, but they don't both come from cows. Putting them in the same section in the grocery store has confused people about the "dairy" status of eggs.

The same thing can happen when we read the Bible. We come to the Bible expecting to find what we've always found. We can easily think parts of the Bible are focused on one thing and entirely miss what they are really talking about.

To see how we can miss the emphasis on joy in God's presence and purposes, let's turn to a verse you might be familiar with, Romans 3:23: "All have sinned and fall short of the glory of God."

We might say this verse is made up of three key ingredients: sin, fall short, and the glory of God. One common way to mix these ingredients is to think of *sin* as "missing the mark or target." *Fall short* is taken as "to fail." These two words mixed together create something like "failing to hit the mark." The *glory of God* is then understood to mean God's righteous law or moral perfection, which, obviously, we have failed to live up to.

So the recipe for these three ingredients looks like this:

- One part *missing the mark* (sin)
- One part *to fail* (fall short)
- One part *God's moral perfection* (the glory of God)

This cooks up a meal of "we have all missed the target, failing God's moral perfection." The implication is clear: we are condemned by God for failing to live up to the good and righteous standard he put in place. This meal can leave a bitter taste in our mouths. It's easy to get the sense that God is angry or disappointed with us.

Of course, we try to remember that "God is love." But after reading this verse, God's love often feels like an afterthought. It feels almost apologetic: "Sorry the meal tastes so horrible. Here's a little ice cream of love to wash it down."

When we read Romans 3:23 according to this recipe, it's hard to comprehend that God loves being *with us*. Instead, it feels like God is all too ready to punish us for failing his standard and merely tolerates us because he has to. Love doesn't seem to be the essence of God. It seems like an afterthought.

Cooking the recipe of Romans 3:23 (and the entire Bible) this way makes for a bitter meal, choked down out of obedience rather than delight. We are hungry and need to eat, and this is the only meal before us.

Is there another way to serve up this verse? Another way to understand the Bible? Another way to experience God?

Lost the Presence and Purposes of God

Let's look at these three ingredients again, but in reverse order.

The *glory of God*, properly understood through the Old Testament, most often refers to the overwhelming display of God's presence. When Scripture speaks of God's glory, the primary meaning is the location of God's presence. Where God's glory is, there God is. In this specific context the glory of God is probably the presence of God experienced by Adam and Eve that was then lost in the fall, coupled with the glory that God gave humanity by making them "in his image."[1]

The second ingredient is *fall short*. A better understanding of this word is "to be lacking or in want of" rather than merely "to fail." John Murray explains that this word refers more to a condition of being (something I *am*) than an action (something I've *done*).[2] Mixing these two ingredients creates the meaning of "lacking the glorious presence of God."

Why do we lack God's presence? Instead of thinking of *sin* as "missing the mark," a better understanding of sin is "stepping off the path" or "veering off the road." God has marked a clear path for us, but we have wandered away from it. Everything on God's path leads to life. And everything off this path leads to death. Sin, therefore, is to walk on the path that leads to death.

So let's rewrite the recipe to look like this:

- One part *God's glorious presence* (glory of God)
- One part *to be lacking* (fall short)
- One part *wandered off the path* (sin)

These three ingredients create a different meal: "All have wandered off God's path of life and now lack God's glorious presence." The accent is now on us wandering away from God, not God rejecting us for our failure. The primary assumption now is that God has created a way—a path, a law—for God and humanity to dwell together in life. And while God desires for humanity to live with God (this is the overlapping of heaven and earth), right now sin prevents that from happening (heaven and earth have been torn apart).

If God longs for us to dwell in his presence and has made a way for us to do this, it becomes much easier to believe God is a God of love. This way of reading Romans 3:23, while different from what we're used to, helps us see that though we have wandered away from God, God still longs for us to dwell in his presence and pursue his purposes.

Our goal throughout is to show that Romans 3:23—and all of Scripture—understands salvation in just this way, and that returning to this path of life returns us not only to God's glorious presence but also to the joy of being with the God who has always wanted to be with us.

Why This Book?

We wrote this book for two reasons. First, you belong in God's presence (*God with us*). Second, you have a place within God's purposes (*God through us*). In other words, God is always glad to be with you and wants nothing more than to draw you closer into his family. And from this place God invites you into the family business, the business of blessing the world. We will see that both of these produce joy in us, a joy matched only by God's joy in us.

We would like to take you on a journey from the beginning to the end of God's work with humanity, from Genesis to Revelation. We'll show you how God continually demonstrates a desire to be with his people—no matter what we do. And we'll highlight the ways God always invites people to join him in his unfolding plan to spread new and unending life throughout the entire world.

Overview

In the chapters to come we'll explore the story of *God with us* and *through us* in four parts: God's idols in creation, God's house in Israel, God's body in Jesus Christ, and God's movement in and through the church.

For those who like all the details: each part has four chapters. The first looks at the big picture of God's work with humanity. The second unfolds how humanity belongs in God's presence (*God with us*) while the third explores how humanity is gathered up into God's purposes for the world (*God through us*). And the last chapter in each part focuses on a defining failure of humanity to live in God's presence and for God's purposes.

At the end of each chapter you'll find (1) a practice to help you build joy and connection with God, (2) a reflection question to help you personalize what you've read in the chapter, (3) a song whose lyrics speak to the theme of the chapter, and (4) an image to help trace the themes of God's presence and purpose through the biblical narrative.

Chapter One

What Is That Smell?

*O*n a trip to France during college, I (Cyd) was walking through a historic garden in Paris with my older sister. Rounding one of the reflecting pools, we both caught a familiar scent and stopped dead in our tracks. "Grandpa and Grandma's backyard in Washington!"

Joy swept over us.

We had no idea what the smell was or where it was coming from, but in a split second we were transported from a thriving metropolitan city in Europe to a quiet backyard in the northwestern corner of the United States. All by a smell.

We searched the gardens and discovered juniper bushes, covered in bright red berries. We bent over and buried our noses in the bushes and began to reminisce about our summers in Washington state, visiting our grandparents. Our bodies were in France, but our minds and our memories were running barefoot through the mowed grass of a small-town backyard where we would salt slugs and lay pennies on the railroad tracks while our grandpa smoked salmon strung up on smoldering cedar planks.

That smell of juniper stirred up memories so sharp and clear that we not only remembered the slugs and the pennies but also the feeling of youthful innocence when we were surrounded by people who loved us and watched over us with great delight as we reveled in the simple pleasures of childhood.

We hadn't been there for more than ten years, and it was over five thousand miles away, but that smell transported us from Paris to Lynden, Washington. We were filled with joy at the memory of being loved in such a lovely place, surrounded by people who were always glad to be with us. Our grandparents delighted in our presence, celebrated our accomplishments, prayed for us daily, played games with us, baked cookies with us, and were always interested in what we were up to. When we were with our grandparents, we were sure we were loved because of the delight they took in being with us. And in response we experienced the joy that came from being with people who were glad to be with us.

This delight, this joy, is what home is all about. It's what we're all looking for. And it's what many of us have never experienced. We're looking for a place to live in the presence of joy and from that place to venture out and contribute to the world. And it's never too late to come home to joy.

This book is about the return home—the return to joy.

The Joy of Creation

Let's start with things at their best. At the beginning all of creation is caught up in the joy of belonging in God's presence. Because God delights in everything he has made, creation responds with joy. The Psalms regularly declare as much.

> The pastures of the wilderness overflow,
>   the hills gird themselves with joy,
>
> the meadows clothe themselves with flocks,
>   the valleys deck themselves with grain,
>   they shout and sing together for joy. (Psalm 65:12-13)
>
> Let the heavens be glad, and let the earth rejoice;
>   let the sea roar, and all that fills it. (Psalm 96:11)

Make a joyful noise to the LORD, all the earth;
  break forth into joyous song and sing praises. (Psalm 98:4)

As the heavens and earth are filled with God's glorious presence, so too the heavens and earth are full of joy and praise.

Joy is the very foundation of reality. Joy is where life began and where life is headed. Creation begins with the joyful communion of God with humanity (the beginning of the book of Genesis), and at the end of all things God and humanity will dwell together again in great joy (the end of the book of Revelation).

Joy is the background music to our lives. It's the soundtrack. It's always there—we just don't always know how to access it. But when we do, joy changes everything. Joy brings us home to the place God made for us.

Joy in the Brain

Joy is woven into the fabric of creation, and it's also wired into our brains. To understand the song of joy as it plays throughout creation, we need to understand a few things about how the brain works and how the capacity—even the necessity—for joy is built into us neurologically.

Humans are born with a fundamental desire to connect with other people. We desire to be wanted, to be delighted in, to be seen and known. We all need the presence of another person. We all crave—neurologically—the experience of joy. In fact, joy can be defined as the experience of being with someone who you feel connected to, someone who is glad to be with you.[1] This will be our definition of joy throughout this book. Tragically, many of us are born into environments that are far from joyful.

Ideally, when a baby is born into a healthy family, she is received with gladness. Her parents look on her with delight and the baby responds with joy. The baby is wanted—is loved. Her parents will make sure she has enough to eat, keep her warm and dry, cuddle her, sing to her, hold her, and play with her. All along the baby's brain is awash in positive neurological activity, activating parts of the brain especially wired to trigger joy in response to other people. Every time the baby feels connected to someone who loves her, she grows stronger in her identity through the experience of joy.

By the time she is three months old, she will have images of her delighted caregiver's face firmly planted in her brain. These wordless images become the foundation for her identity. When she becomes distressed, her caregiver is there—even if just as a memory.[2] From comfort to a difficult situation and back to comfort, the baby's neural pathways are learning how to return to the joy of connection amid distress. This process can be called "returning to joy."

During this early journey from distress and back to joy, the baby is internalizing some important things. Even in her preverbal state the tiny child knows that someone sees her, hears her crying, and understands what she is experiencing. Someone is glad to be with her and does whatever is needed to alleviate her distress (changing her diaper, feeding her, cuddling her, or rocking her to sleep). This empathy and attention are referred to as attunement.

Over time this process creates neural pathways capable of carrying the child out of pain and returning her to joy. As this happens over and over again the child internalizes that she is seen, heard, and understood. Eventually, even when her caregiver is not present, she can return to joy just by thinking of and remembering being loved.

Exploring from Joy

Children—and then adults—with a firm foundation of joy also have the capacity to make positive contributions in the world. It starts with play and exploration. When a child has a firm foundation of joy, then, little by little, the child will adventure further and further into the world (even if it is just a new toy or the next room over). The bumps and bruises of exploration are overcome by being able to return to joy (either through the physical presence or the memory of a safe person).

A child with a firm foundation of joy assumes the world is a fundamentally safe place, even if it is punctured by occasional pain or distress. As the child grows into adulthood, their exploration and play turn into the courage and creativity to contribute to the world in a positive way.

Our brains are wired for joy. They are conditioned for connection.

Relational Experiences: Joy and Shame

Joy is fundamentally a relational experience. Joy requires other people. You can't experience joy without another person present or without at least thinking about another person.

Sadly, many of us don't get a joyful start to life. For some of us our caretakers were absent or distracted. We grew up in a stressful or dangerous environment, or in a home or neighborhood where basic necessities were absent. We grew up learning that no one was there to hear us, no one sees what we need, and no one will act on our behalf. Or worse, we learn that the people who are supposed to care for us actually despise us.

This brings us to shame, the shadow side of joy. Shame is the experience of being with someone who is not glad to be with us. Shame is feeling disconnected from someone who isn't glad to be with us. Sometimes we feel shame because we sin and, as a result, we break our relationships with others and so experience disconnection.

But sometimes the disconnection is not our fault. We experience abuse, neglect, intense anger, and unearned disgust from others. In these situations we still experience a disconnection, even if the disconnection is not a result of our own sin. Although shame is often connected to our sin, shame can also be experienced because of someone else's sin coming at us.

Without healthy and loving relationships, it is difficult to experience joy and easy to experience shame. Many of us never had these healthy relationships. And many of us don't have much joy in our lives. We carry loads of shame instead.

Often our attempts to manage shame lead us into deeper sin and further away from joyful relationships. But that doesn't change the fact that we are driven by the desire to be in the presence of someone who is glad to be with us: the desire to be wanted, to be connected. And we search for these connections everywhere we go. When we don't find them in relationships, we look for them in things—in chocolate, wine, distractions, and addictions. But these aren't capable of building joy. They are false substitutes. And our world is saturated with the smell of false joy, fake belonging, and artificial connection. The joy of creation and our certainty of belonging with God are drowned out by the stench of sin and shame.

Identity and Joy

Let's get back to the brain for a moment. Joy is experienced in the same part of the brain where our sense of identity is built.[3] When someone has a strong foundation of joy, he knows who he is. He is the same person when he is angry, sad, afraid, or glad. His emotions do not change his understanding of himself or the way others experience him. He has a steady sense of self and does not need to pretend to be someone he's not. Because he feels safe and strong, he can be himself.

Conversely, someone who does not have a strong foundation of joy has a fragile identity. It will seem like he changes into a different person when he is overwhelmed by negative emotions. The person you thought you knew will disappear and someone else seems to take his place—even if for just a moment. He will lose himself in these emotions, and you'll wonder how he can be capable of such different kinds of behaviors.

Joy is the foundation of our identity and our resilience. Our neural pathways are wired as a result of our early experiences of joy. Without a strong foundation of joy, we struggle for identity and are crippled by shame. It's no wonder Scripture declares, "The joy of the LORD is [my] strength" (Nehemiah 8:10).

The good news is that our brains are changeable. It's never too late to connect with someone who is glad to be with you and to experience the joy of that connection. When this happens, new neural pathways are formed. Your brain can be literally "transformed by the renewing of your minds" (Romans 12:2).

Presence and Purpose

Springing from a foundation of joy is the capacity for creative contribution. The joyful presence of one person gives us the ability to pursue creative work on behalf of other people—passing along both joy and love. If we feel we belong, then we will be free to bless others.

Presence and purpose. Connection and contribution. Belonging and blessing. These are the fundamental notes of joy that will sound throughout this book.

Because everything already belongs in God's presence, joy is the natural state of all things. When we listen closely, the sound underneath everything that exists is the song of joy. Joy is the song sung in response to God's presence, the one who is glad to be with us, and with all of his creation.

Practice: Finding Your Joy Place

Think back over your life and try to remember a place where you felt safe and at peace, a time when you felt relaxed and okay. It could be an outdoor place—like on a beach or sitting in a tree. Maybe it's an indoor place like a quiet reading chair or a kitchen table. Close your eyes and remember this place as completely as you can. Imagine yourself being there, noticing the sights, sounds, feels, smells, tastes. Notice what it feels like in your body to be there. Spend a minute enjoying this place using your imagination. Notice what it feels like to be safe and at peace. Then take some time to thank God for this place, no matter how small or normal it might seem.

Reflection

Remember the last time you were with someone who was glad to be with you.

How did the person greet you?

How could you tell that they were glad to be with you?

What was it like to be together?

This is what joy feels like.

Song

Listen to "Joy" by Rend Collective. Will you open yourself again to the hope of joy?

PLACE of JOY

Creation is a place of joy, where God is "glad to be with us."

Part One

God's Idols

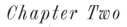

Chapter Two

Where Is Home?

About a month away from our first son's due date, we were preparing to move into the church parsonage. On a Sunday evening in late June we walked around the empty house, spackling holes, taping off ceilings and floor boards, and making plans to paint walls. In the morning we would open the paint cans and get started.

But God had other plans. A little after midnight we were on our way to the hospital instead. Soren was born the next morning, four weeks early!

Nothing in our old apartment was packed. Nothing in the new house was ready. And now we had a new baby to look after. With no home to go home to, Cyd and baby Soren headed to a hotel. Right at the beginning of our new life as a family, we were temporarily homeless. It was totally disorienting.

This experience matched the disorientation we would feel fifteen years later.

During the summer of 2018, we were fully immersed in our life as a family (now with two boys). But God changed everything again. After a six-week whirlwind, we discerned with friends and the Holy Spirit that God was moving us from Chicago to Grand Rapids, Michigan.

With the help of both our old and new communities, we were able to buy a house in Grand Rapids. As part of the sale, we agreed to allow the seller to stay in the house for thirty days after closing. So when we moved on Labor Day weekend to begin work at our new church, our house wasn't ready for us. Fortunately, a friend of a friend offered to let us stay in his cottage on Lake Michigan.

The time in the cottage started off great—enjoying the beach, kayaking, gorgeous sunsets, stunning moonrises—but after two weeks we were getting anxious to move into our own house. We had left a home we'd lived in for fifteen years and a church we'd attended for seventeen. We felt uprooted, disoriented, and disconnected. We wanted to be home. We longed for a place where we could set a table for new friends and neighbors.

Hard to Come By

We all live in a transitive world. People transfer to new cities for their jobs, upgrade to bigger homes, downsize to smaller apartments, or get new roommates. The days of growing up in a single home with your grandparents living just down the street have faded.

These days a sense of home is hard to come by. Many of us go about our days living in places we know are temporary, on our way to something else. We're more disconnected from our families than at any other time in human history and more on the move. We are more virtual and less face-to-face. It's harder and harder to find places of belonging and connection than ever before. We long for a place where we feel rooted, grounded, at home.

The good news is that we always have a home with God. In fact, all of creation is the house God built to make a home for his family. And God always intended to move in—to live with his family. God wanted to build a place that would become the foundation for joy—the place where humanity would know security in being known and loved by God, and from this place to venture out and contribute to blessing God's creation.

Reading Backward

The idea that the heavens and earth are God's home is woven into the story of creation, found in Genesis 1–3.

Sometimes when people are learning to draw, they are asked to sketch familiar objects upside down and told to focus on the spaces between things. The idea is to get past the normal expectations and see something new, something that has always been there. The story of creation may be so familiar to you that you haven't read it recently. But we want to urge you to look again—to approach this story from a different angle and see what you may have missed.

While it would be difficult to read Genesis 1–3 upside down, we are going to read it backward. We'll see how everything was made as a home for God to live in: a home where joy would spring forth from the relationship between God, the good and loving Father, and his children.

Not Just a Garden

If you were to go to work today and you found the place surrounded by the Secret Service, what would you think? Most people would assume the president of the United States was somewhere nearby. Why? Because the main job of the Secret Service is to protect the president. They are his security guards. Wherever the Secret Service is, you can bet the president is nearby.

When we look at Genesis 3:24 we find the exact same thing: God's security guards.

Let's look at the whole verse: "[God] drove out the man; and at the east of the garden of Eden he placed the cherubim, and a sword flaming and turning to guard the way to the tree of life."

God placed a specific kind of angel (cherubim) at the entrance of the Garden, to guard the way back in. Why is this significant?

Cherubim are especially associated with God's presence. They are God's Secret Service agents. Whenever we find cherubim in the Bible, God is nearby. So if we find cherubim guarding the entrance to the

Garden of Eden, that means they are guarding access to the very presence of God, to God's home.

Now let's move back to Genesis 2. Unlike the president, who's generally inaccessible to normal people, God is not a distant government official. It might seem startling that God regularly walked and talked with Adam and Eve in the Garden of Eden. But we won't be surprised if we understand that God made the Garden to be his family home where he would live with his children (Genesis 2:8).

The Garden of Eden was created to be God's house. He always intended to live there with his people. We know this because there are so many parallels between the Garden and the later temple in Jerusalem. Usually what we call the home of God (or a god) is a temple. Sometimes we think of a temple as the place to make sacrifices—the place God deals with our sins. That is true in a sense. But in the ancient world, a temple was first and foremost the home of a particular god. Even in the Bible, the whole point of the temple in Jerusalem was for God and humanity to live together as a family.

In Genesis 2—in the Garden of Eden—we find important symbols that reappear in the tabernacle and the temple of God. In fact, the later tabernacle and temple are copies of the original, the Garden of Eden.[1] Here are some of the parallels:

- God walks in the Garden: The only other times God is said to walk with his people is in the tabernacle (Leviticus 26:11-12).
- The Garden's entrance faced east, just like the later tabernacle and the temple (Genesis 3:24; Ezekiel 40:6).
- The Garden was full of gold and precious stones (Genesis 2:11-12). The tabernacle and the temple were also adorned with these (Genesis 2:12; Exodus 25: 7, 11-39; 28: 6-27; 1 Kings 6:20-21).
- God placed Adam and Eve in the Garden to "cultivate and keep" it. The only other times these two words are used together is when the Bible is talking about the work of the priests in the temple (Numbers 3:7-8; 8:25-26; 18:5-6; 1 Chronicles 23:32; Ezekiel 44:14).

But God's presence wasn't limited to just the Garden. As we move back from Genesis 2 to Genesis 1, we see that all of creation is God's home.

Not How Long but What

When we read Genesis 1, we can get distracted by *how* questions: How long did it take God to create the world (literal twenty-four-hour days or metaphorical spans of time)? How old is the earth? How did God do it all? All these questions focus on the *how* of God's creation. But too often these questions cause us to miss the importance of *what* and *why* God created.

The number seven offers an insight.

The only other places in the Old Testament where the number seven is mentioned so often is the construction of the tabernacle and temple. The seven days of creation ("God said, 'Let there be . . .'") are paralleled by the seven different instructions God gives Moses for building the tabernacle ("The Lord said . . ."). And when Solomon built the temple it took him seven years. He finished on the seventh month of the year, during the seven-day-long Feast of Booths. And his prayer of dedication for the temple has seven petitions.[2]

The importance of seven in the creation of heaven and earth *and* in the construction of the tabernacle and temple suggest that creation itself is the original temple for God.

And how do we know that God lives in this cosmic temple of heaven and earth?

Because of what happens on the seventh day.

Ready to Move In

But before we get to the seventh day, let's go back to the first moving story we told—the one when our son was born four weeks early.

After Soren's surprise birth on that Monday, our church jumped into action. Some people helped pack up the old apartment. Others helped paint the rooms in the new house. Some brought food for Cyd and Soren. Six days later, our church helped us move everything in. By that time we were exhausted from constantly running around from the hospital to the new house, from the old apartment to the hotel. We were tired of getting ready, tired of being in limbo. By Saturday it was time to move in.

And we were more than ready. It was time to stop preparing to live as a family and actually start living! It was time to make this house a home. And we did!

We spent fifteen amazing years growing our family in that house—bringing our second son, Tennyson, home only seventeen months later. Our house was filled with the shrieks of wrestle time, the giggles of tickling and ridiculous jokes, the painful sounds of beginner instruments, the music of worship, the chatter of gathered friends and family, and deep connections with our neighbors. It was a home filled with joy—a place where we could be glad to be with one another, a place for joyful connections and a home base for creative adventures.

On a much grander level we see the same thing happening in the first chapter of Genesis. All of creation is like a new house where God lives—a place specially prepared for God, his people, and all of creation to live together! It's a house that will be filled with joy—where God is glad to be with his children. It was also intended to be a place where everyone and everything was drawn into that joy of connection. We see this clearly when God rests on the seventh day.

Where Does God Rest?

Normally we think of the seventh day of creation as the day when nothing happened. God rested (Genesis 2:2). And God gave us the day of rest—the sabbath—because of this (Exodus 20:11).

But if we only think of the seventh day as the day God ceased working, we'll miss something essential. We need to ask, Where does God rest? and What does resting really mean?

Resting seems to happen best in a certain place. Some people have a favorite chair for reading at the end of the day or a porch swing on which to welcome the evening. Some love walking or hiking. Others snuggle under blankets to watch a movie. With throw pillows, blankets, and a hammock, our son Tennyson has created the perfect place for listening to audiobooks—a little retreat center from the bustle of the house.

In the same way, throughout the Bible we're told *where* God rests. God rests in the tabernacle or temple. In this case, resting doesn't mean lounging around and doing nothing. It means that God is present there. In the ancient world people believed that the god they worshiped actually lived in the temple. That's why they would offer sacrifices and worship in a temple—they believed they were in the presence of their god, in the god's house.

Israel's understanding of God was no different. In Psalm 132, worshipers are called to go up to God's "resting place" to worship. This resting place also happens to be God's dwelling place (vv. 7-8). But, as Isaiah reminds us, God doesn't merely rest or dwell in the temple made by humans. Instead, he says,

> Heaven is my throne
>> and the earth is my footstool.
> what is the house that you would build for me?
>> and what is my resting place? (Isaiah 66:1)

All of creation is God's resting place. And as God's resting place, creation is also God's dwelling place—his home. So when Genesis 2:2 says God rested on the seventh day, it means God moved into his house.

When Soren was born early, we spent an entire week getting our new house in order—packing, painting, and moving. But the point of all that was so we could begin the joyful work of raising our family. After all this work we finally rested from preparing—in our new home. And for fifteen years after that, we were engaged in the joyful work of living as a family and inviting others to share our joy.

The seven days of creation tell the same story—the story of God creating a world he could rest in, a world made as a home for his family. And God didn't move in so he could just sit around. He moved in to start living as the Father of his new family and as the King of creation.

Creation is God's house, the place of his presence. The heavens and the earth are the home of God. In God's house humanity was given access to God's presence (*God with us*) and a share in God's purposes in the world (*God through us*). God's house was meant to be the foundation of joy, a foundation that would establish loving connections from which we could make creative contributions.

Not Home Yet

And yet many of us don't feel at home in creation or in God's presence. We are still looking for home.

After fifteen years in our first house, we were called away. We finally moved into our new home on the last day of September 2018.

As I (Cyd) write this in December of 2018, our new house still doesn't feel like home. It feels like someone else's house. It feels borrowed, temporary, and a little surreal. It will never be the sweet little parsonage I took my babies home to where they learned to walk and talk and read. The shrieks and giggles of wrestle time will never fill our new living room here. There won't be backyard fires, clucking chickens, and, most notably, my neighbor Dale doesn't live next door to us anymore. Even as I write this, I'm trying to hold back tears—the longing for the sense of rootedness and home that comes from fifteen years of memories and neighboring cannot be easily replaced. When I used to walk in the door of our old house after a long trip, I would breathe a huge sigh of relief and say, "It's good to be home." But that hasn't happened yet in our new house.

We all have a deep ache for home—a place full of joyful connections and creative contributions. A place we know we belong and a place from which we can bless others. But before we talk about why we all have this deep ache, we need to look at what God made us to be—his "images" in the world.

Practice: Enjoying God's Gift To You

Go back to the place you imagined in the last chapter. We're going to refer to this place as your "joy place." Remember the sights, smells, tastes, feels, and sounds. God created the heavens and the earth so he could be with his creation. God designed this place too. Can you enjoy this place as a gift from God? Enjoy his creativity in this place. Notice his attention to detail. Notice what it feels like to be in this joy place.

Reflection

What feels like home for you?

How do you know when you're feeling at home?

How do you try to make others feel at home?

Do you feel at home with God?

Song

Listen to "Belong" by Chris Rice. Can you relate to the longing for a place to belong?

God and humanity experience joy together as heaven (God's place) and earth (humanity's place) overlap.

Chapter Three

Do I Belong Here?

*O*ur two black cats, Johnny and June, have become examples of the
difference that belonging makes. June is timid, skittish, fearful.
She will only approach us when the house is quiet, no one is moving
around, and we've been sitting in the same spot for several minutes.
When she does decide to emerge from the shadows, she will come
near and meow tentatively—but as soon as we move she runs away.
She repeats this pattern several times every evening. If we don't look
at her directly, don't move in her direction, in fact, if we don't move at
all, then she will draw near and even sit in a lap.

She doesn't trust that she's welcome. She's always afraid we're going
to turn against her and shoo her away. She doesn't believe she belongs
with us. She doesn't believe that we like having her around.

Johnny, on the other hand, knows he belongs. He trusts his place
in our house. He sprawls in the middle of the coffee table and jumps
on the chairs around the kitchen table as if he's joining us for dinner.
He confidently climbs on our laps the moment we sit down, and he
leaps into our bed hoping we'll let him sleep with us (which we don't—
he has the habit of sleeping on our faces). He knows he belongs. He
assumes he's welcome. He knows we like having him around.

Many of us can relate to June. In our lives at work, at home, with
our families, or among strangers, we are constantly testing the waters,

tentatively coming out of our shell but just as quick to hide again. Sure, some of us might come across like Johnny, confidently strutting around like we own the place. But often beneath the surface is the fear of loneliness, the struggle for acceptance, and the longing to belong.

In chapter two we saw that God created the heavens and the earth to be his dwelling place, a cosmic temple where he would rest and rule all things. Heaven and earth are God's home.

But does God want anyone else in his home? Would God be happier if everyone would just leave him alone and stop making so many messes? Is God a hermit living alone in the wild, a recluse who keeps to himself?

Of course not!

God made this world as a home to be shared with his children. We know this because God created humanity in his "image and likeness," as part of his family—living in his home. In other words, God is a father providing a good home for his children. Humanity was created to live in God's presence. This is the foundation of *God with us*.

Do you believe you are welcome in God's home? Do you act like Johnny who believes he belongs? Or are you more like June, always afraid of getting kicked out?

Mirror, Mirror in the World

What does being made in God's image really mean? And how does this help us know we belong in God's presence?

Every era of human history (at least in the West) idealized something about humanity, and then—presto!—we assumed that's what it means to be made in the image of God. In ancient times when people generally thought of the material world as unimportant, people believed our spiritual nature made us like God. Later thinkers taught that unlike the beasts, humanity's capacity for reason made us like God. During the Industrial Revolution our ability to create and produce reflected the image of God. More recently our social ability makes us like God.

But the problem isn't deciding which part reflects the image of God, our spirituality, rationality, productivity, or connectivity. We are like God in all these ways. The problem is the idea of *reflecting* God. The idea assumes we are like a mirror that bounces God's image into the world.[1]

This mirror metaphor is unhelpful for two reasons.

First, the idea that we are mirrors reflecting God into the world places a separation between God and the rest of creation. If we are only reflecting God, then God is not really present or available to us.[2] But God is not distant and impersonal, as we'll see.

Second, and more importantly, the idea of a mirror doesn't convey the true meaning of the Hebrew word in Genesis 1:26—that we have been made in the "image" of God.

A Living Idol?

Although you wouldn't know it from most English translations, the Hebrew word translated as "image" in Genesis 1 is usually translated in the rest of the Bible as "idol," as in those carved representations of gods placed in temples—those things that Israel is forbidden to make or worship![3]

With such a negative meaning it's no wonder translators leaned toward a more neutral word like *image*. Why would humanity be created as the idol of God? That sounds blasphemous!

But if we want to be true to the meaning of a word—if we are attempting to be true to the Bible—then humanity *is* God's idol, placed inside the temple of creation.

In fact, the creation of humans in Genesis 2 strongly resembles the manufacturing of idols in Egypt and Mesopotamia. "Then the LORD God *formed man from the dust* of the ground, and *breathed into his nostrils* the breath of life; and the man became a living being. . . . The LORD God *took the man and put him* in the garden of Eden to till it and keep (Genesis 2:7, 15, emphasis added).

In these verses God forms humanity from the dust of the earth, breathes life into us, and places us in a garden. All of these actions have parallels with how pagan priests would create idols of false gods. God forms humanity out of the earth—just as a priest would sculpt clay to fashion an idol. God breathes into the nostrils of humanity—just as a pagan priest would breathe on the faces of the idols to "animate" them. And God places Adam in a garden—a garden that we already know is like a temple—just as ancient priests installed their idol in the temple of their god (of course we need to remember that the creation, animation, and installation of false idols is a distant echo and distortion of God's true creation of humanity—not the other way around).[4]

But why does the priest install idols in the temple anyway? What was their purpose?

Idols are a tangible representation of the character and attributes of the god. They give a concrete shape to the abstract presence of the deity. They embody the presence of the god.

Tangible Image

We see this at work in the story of the false god Dagon and God's ark of the covenant in 1 Samuel 4–6.

Placed in the center of the tabernacle and later the temple, the ark of the covenant—a huge, ornate box—represented the center of God's presence with Israel. Carved onto the lid of the ark were golden sculptures of cherubim—God's Secret Service agents, the ones that protected his presence. These cherubim reminded Israel that the ark was the exact place of God's presence.

One day the Philistines—Israel's sworn enemies—attacked and captured the ark of God. This was a dark day for Israel. The ark was so important to Israel that a woman giving birth on the day of the attack named her son Ichabod, which means "The glory has departed from Israel" (1 Samuel 4:21-22).

The triumphant Philistines brought the ark back to the temple of their god, Dagon. They placed it at the foot of the idol to show that Israel's God had been defeated by Dagon and now had to bow at Dagon's feet.

But the next morning, to their surprise, the Philistines found that the idol of Dagon had fallen over on his face before the ark of God. They set their idol on its feet again, but the next morning they found him in the same position again. But this time his head and his hands were broken off. This was serious business! Instead of God bowing in submission to Dagon, it was Dagon—in Dagon's own house!—who was bowing before God.

The situation was not lost on the Philistines. "The ark of the God of Israel must not remain with us, for his hand is heavy on us and on our god Dagon" (1 Samuel 5:7). The idol of Dagon, which represented Dagon's presence, was broken before the presence of the true God.

Dagon's idol fell before God. And the Philistines understood that not just the idol—the physical representation—was in trouble. Dagon himself was in trouble. They were all in trouble.

This story reminds us that idols are so much more than mirrors reflecting the presence of a god. If the mirror of a telescope is broken, that doesn't mean the light from a star no longer shines. There is no real connection between the star and the mirror. The mirror simply reflects the light given by the stars, and if the mirror breaks, it can be replaced.

Not so with an idol. The idol is so connected to the presence of the one it images that when the idol is knocked over or destroyed, the deity itself is affected.

Attuned to God

In chapter one we talked about joy as a relational experience. God created humans to be in relationship, and as relational beings we are capable of nonverbal communication. We communicate with tone of voice, body language, facial expressions, even intangible vibes that we pick up from another person nearby. This all happens because our brains have what are called "mirror neurons." These neurons allow us to pick up and reflect nonverbal communication much faster than verbal communication. Because of this we are more attuned to people (their moods and emotions) through what their bodies express than through their words. Likewise, because of these mirror neurons, we are much more likely to mirror the emotions and behaviors of people around us without even being aware of it. In this way our neural pathways mimic (or mirror) the neural pathways of other people. It is how we stay connected, both emotionally and relationally.[5]

As idols of God, as image bearers, we are connected to the presence of God. God is with us. When we are connected with God, our mirror neurons are attuned to God—attuned to what he is thinking and feeling about us, others, and the world. Through this attunement with God, we bear his presence to everything in the world.

Dwelling Presence

As strange as it might sound, humanity *is* the idol of God, created by God and attuned to his presence.

Have you ever wondered why God was so adamant about the prohibition against idols in the Old Testament? It isn't just a matter of worshiping something besides God. God commanded Israel not to have or worship any idols because there already were idols made in the image of God—humans. Humanity was God's idol in the world. To say "you are the hands and feet of God" is not just a figure of speech. You actually are the tangible presence of God. Humanity is as closely related to God as the idol of Dagon was to Dagon.

The implications for this connection are truly staggering.

First, we belong in the presence of God. We are welcome before God. We don't need to be afraid to draw near to God. God created us to be with him, to always know and be known in his presence. God designed us to experience his delight in us. We don't need to wonder if we are a bother or a hassle. God wants to be near us. It is what we were created for.

Second, God actually likes you. If you belong with God, if you were created to be in his presence, then this means God actually likes you! Let that sink in. God doesn't merely put up with you. God doesn't just tolerate you. You aren't placed in a corner and forgotten. You are made for God's presence. You are made to live and dwell with God.

You are made in God's image—you belong in the family. God is our Father and we are his children. And we are the "apple of his eye" (Psalm 17:8)—the best part of everything he made.

Believing We Belong

Can we really believe God wants to be with us?

In a sense this is the essence of faith—believing that we belong in the Father's presence. Later we will see that Adam and Eve were tempted to stop believing they belonged with God. Forgetting to believe this—losing faith—opened the door to sin and shame.

How would your life change if you truly believed you belonged in God's presence? How might it change the way you approach God? What would feel different if you believed God made you to be with him and that you are welcome in his presence *all the time*—not because of anything you've done, not because you say the right words or act the right way, but because you are made in his image and you belong in his presence?

How might it feel to never wonder whether God would shoo you away? If you never questioned whether he is annoyed with you or not? What new risks might you be willing to take if you knew you could never lose God's love, never disappoint him, never fail to live up to his expectations for you? What relational security might it bring you to know that someone is always glad to be with you and you can always "return to joy" in his presence?

From Presence to Purpose

But God didn't create us just to hang out. We were made to be with God, but that isn't our entire purpose. We belong in God's presence (*God with us*). And from God's presence we also become a blessing to all of God's creation (*God through us*).

Practice: Enjoying Belonging

Go back to your joy place. Spend time remembering all the details again. The more often you remember this place (and others like it), you will find that it comes back more quickly and with less work. This time, as you imagine yourself there, remember that you belong in God's presence. If God were present in this joy place, where might he be? He might be sitting or standing, moving or still. He might be near to you or farther away. Imagine him there with you. Imagine him enjoying how much you enjoy this place that he made. Notice what this feels like. In a very real sense, this is *faith*—believing that you belong in God's presence.

Reflection

As you think of yourself as God's idol, does anything shift in your thinking about yourself?

Which of our cats do you most identify with? Johnny, who knows he belongs? Or June, who is always wondering?

What keeps you from believing you belong in God's presence?

Song

While listening to "Hands of God" by Francesca Battistelli, think about how we minister the presence of God to each other.

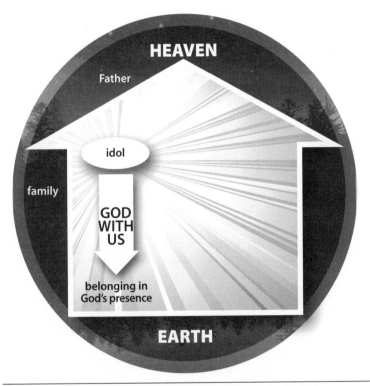

As family, we belong in our Father's house. As his idols, God places us within the temple of creation (his house).

Chapter Four

Does My Work Matter?

*A*m I adding anything meaningful to the world? Do I have something significant to contribute? It may sound nice that we were created to dwell in God's presence, but what else am I supposed to do with my life?

I (Cyd) struggled with thoughts of insignificance when I first started staying at home after Soren was born. At first, I enjoyed the reprieve from a job. I didn't have to dress up, deal with a lot of people, pack a lunch, or drive anywhere. I could stay in my pajamas if I wanted to! I could read books, take naps—it was almost like a vacation. But the initial excitement about the change of pace quickly became a sense of just drifting through life. A cloud of purposelessness started gathering around me. Yes, my purpose was to feed, diaper, and soothe our son, to make sure he had everything he needed to grow up healthy and strong. But compared to the kinds of work I had done in the past, it felt pretty insignificant. Everything I did was for one person—one who wasn't even capable of appreciating my efforts.

I longed to pour myself into meaningful work, to make a difference, to change the world. Had I known everything I know now about how brains develop and how crucial it is to build joy as a foundation for infants, I might have felt differently about staying home with our kids.

But as it was, I viewed that season primarily by how it affected my life rather than the impact it was having on the tiny humans I was sharing life with. The sheer monotony of the repetitive tasks seemed to drown out any sense of significance. It felt like I was spinning my wheels, watching the world go by. I felt as if life was on hold until I could return to doing something that really mattered.

Does My Work Matter?

Many of us have experienced the fatigue of monotonous tasks and the emotional drain of wondering if any of it really matters. Some of us have experienced the disorientation of being out of work—whether we lost a job, can't find a job, or chose to be away from a job for a season. Maybe your joblessness has caused you to question your worth or to wonder if you have anything to offer the world at all.

Maybe you've never experienced a season of your life when you questioned your purpose. Maybe you've always known how significant your work is. If that's the case, celebrate!

But maybe you still wonder if your work matters *to God.* Maybe you wonder if your success is in line with God's work in the world. Maybe you even wonder if your work has become an idol in your life—more important than your devotion to God and his purposes in the world.

Regardless of what your experience has been or currently is, the reality is that we're invited to participate in God's meaningful work. We have a purpose, and it's very real and terribly significant. We bear the image of the living God (and in so doing, we bring him honor or disgrace). We are part of God's family—and there is a family business to run.

Images Rule

In chapter three we only gave you half of what it means to be made in the image of God. We explored what it means to be tangible idols of God, living in and representing God's presence in the world. We were created for the joy of dwelling with God (*God with us*).

But being made in God's image is also about God's *purposes* in the world (*God through us*). In order to understand how image is connected with purpose, we need to understand a common practice in the ancient world.

Since the end of the Second World War in 1945, North Korea has been ruled by the Kim family. Kim Il Sung and then his son Kim Jong Il ruled for over sixty-six years, demanding total loyalty and even veneration. To this day pictures of these leaders are hung in just about every home, office building, and school. There are over five hundred statues of Kim Il Sung all around North Korea. Kim Il Sung's grandson, Kim Jong Un, assumed power in 2011 and is now building three enormous statues on the highest mountain in North Korea as a tribute to himself, his father, and his grandfather. These pictures and statues are constant reminders to the people of North Korea that the Kims are in charge and demand their loyalty.

In the same way, to show where they ruled and reigned, kings in the ancient world set up giant statues of themselves. The kings placed these images in the center of their cities and at the borders of their lands to remind people who was in charge. As we said in chapter three, an image isn't something we look at on a screen, a reflection in a mirror, or picture seen with the eyes. *Image* refers to a statue or a figure that can be touched—something we can't ignore.

In the ancient world it was understood that a god would have a living image of himself in the world. But the living image only applied to one person: the king! Egyptian and Babylonian kings—and they alone—were called the image of god. Because the king was the god's image in the world, the king was also the rightful ruler of the kingdom, and he set up images of himself to remind everyone that he alone was in charge.

Great for the king. Bad for everyone else.

All of Humanity Rules!

But God didn't think only one person should rule his creation: instead, he put all people in charge of creation. It must have been quite a shock for ancient readers to hear these words from Genesis 1:27:

> So God created humankind in his image,
>   in the image of God he created them;
>   male and female he created them.

All of humanity is God's image. Not just one person. Not just the king.

And if all of humanity is made in God's image, then all are meant to share in God's royal rule of the world. God has placed humanity at the center and on the border of his kingdom as living images of God's rule in the world. Every human is empowered by God, the King, to extend his rule and reign in the world. Every human is an ambassador of the King's reign.

Maybe you are thinking this is too much to get out of just one word. And maybe it would be if the surrounding verses didn't say exactly the same thing. Genesis 1:26 says God created humanity to have dominion over all the animals of the seas, in the air, and on the ground. And verse 28 says humanity would fill and subdue the earth.

Humanity—God's image in the world—is supposed to rule over all creation, acting as agents or representatives of God's kingdom in the world. And through humanity, acting on behalf of God, the true King, all of life would be blessed and flourish. Humanity was created to be the conduit of blessing—from God to all the world.

The Flow of Blessing

We recently flew to the Bay Area to visit my (Geoff's) hometown of San Jose to surf in Santa Cruz, where Cyd and I met, and to spend a couple of days hanging out in San Francisco.

Flying over the Central Valley of California, the boys eyed a wide highway cutting through the landscape. But they also noticed another highway, running parallel to it. Why were there two highways so close together, traveling in the same direction?

We eventually figured out that the second one wasn't a highway at all. It was an aqueduct. Aqueducts bring water from the slopes of the Sierra Nevada Mountains in Northern California to the desert basin of Southern California. This four-hundred-mile system of aqueducts, tunnels, and pumping stations brings one of the necessities of life to Southern California. Without water there would be no Los Angeles, no Hollywood, no nothing in Southern California. Without it the whole bottom half of the state would shrivel up and die.

Just like these water channels, humanity is supposed to be God's aqueducts, allowing blessing to flow through us into all creation. Wherever humanity goes, the flow of life and blessing were meant to follow. The blessing of God's kingdom was supposed to spring up wherever humanity lived. "God blessed them, and God said to them, 'Be fruitful and multiply, and fill the earth and subdue it; and have dominion over the fish of the sea and over the birds of the air and over every living thing that moves upon the earth'" (Genesis 1:28).

God blessed his living images to be fruitful and to multiply, and to use their authority on behalf of the King to care for all the living creatures—to make sure that everything along the aqueduct of blessing received what it needed to flourish. When humanity does this, the earth will fill up with little living images who represent God's rule in the world. And when the earth is full of these living images of God's rule, then they will quite naturally have dominion over all things, just like God does.

Dominion Is Not What You Think!

I (Geoff) have three siblings—a twin brother and an older sister and brother. Four is the perfect number for playing cards. We loved playing cards together. Or rather, I loved playing when I didn't lose!

I vividly remember one day throwing my cards down and storming out of the room yelling, "I hate this game!" It's probably such a vivid memory because it happened all the time! I would lose and storm off. My siblings dominated me in cards, and I hated it.

To this day, whenever I get together with family I know my older brother Sebastian and my brother-in-law, Charlie, will own me whenever we play cards. I just can't beat them, ever! They totally dominate me—and no, I'm not exaggerating. (Thankfully I don't storm out of the room anymore.)

Total victory over a competitor. A demonstration of power over someone else. This is what we usually think when we hear of domination. Often this is what we think of when we hear that humanity is supposed to subdue and have dominion over the earth. If this were true, then it would be a pretty awful way for humanity to relate to God's creation, tending toward abuse and exploitation.

But our dominion over God's creation is not a license to abuse or exploit it. We don't get to do whatever we want with the resources of the world just because we are made in God's image. We aren't setting up our own rule and reign. We are partnering with God in his rule and reign, and this means allowing life and blessing to flow through us. God placed Adam and Eve in the Garden and charged them with the task of tending and keeping it. You don't care for a garden by ruthlessly dominating it but by cultivating it so that it becomes more productive and more beautiful.

Tending and Keeping

Cultivating soil and growing plants is a process of tending and keeping, a continual work of subduing the unruly parts and helping the growing parts to flourish. Our neighbor Dale and I (Cyd) grew a garden together for years. In the beginning, when we decided where to put our garden, we had to cut back the sod and till the soil. You might imagine this was a one-time effort. But it's not! If we're not diligent with weeding, the weeds quickly take over. Not only that but the plants themselves will encroach on each other, choking out the life of their neighbors. Watermelon vines will creep into the corn, tomatoes will overwhelm the peppers, and kale will take over the kohlrabi.

But all the tilling and weeding and tending are done for the purpose of blessing. I like to think about how to make all the plants in the garden happy. A happy plant is doing what it's created to do. This requires tending to the needs of each plant. If you try to grow watermelon like you grow lettuce, for example, you're in for disaster. We plant our lettuce seeds in shallow soil with about a hundred seeds in a short, little row. Because the roots aren't that deep and we harvest it frequently, it doesn't require much space. Watermelon, on the other hand, needs room. We plant four seedlings in a mound about six to eight feet apart from any other plants. As it grows, the vines spread along the ground and take up all the available space.

Trying to train watermelon to grow in neat little lettuce rows would be a waste of time and effort. You can't dominate the watermelon and make it bend to your will. Instead, you have to cooperate with how it's meant to grow. If you don't tend it properly, it won't produce any fruit. If we tend all the plants well, if we *subdue* them, they become happy, productive, fruitful plants. If we don't, they grow wild and disorganized and bear little to no fruit. Our *rule* over the garden creates flourishing—every plant growing according to its design and producing bountiful fruit. When the garden does well, there is plenty to share with others.

When God gave Adam and Eve dominion over all living things, he was giving them the responsibility to pay attention to how each thing was designed, what it needed to grow, and how to help it produce its specific fruit. Our dominion over God's creation was always intended to be of this kind. Adam and Eve were given the privilege of being conduits of God's blessing—to make sure everything received what it needed so that it could join in the song of joy that all of creation was intended to sing.

Growing the Garden

So here's a question: If Adam and Eve were placed in the Garden, blessed and told to be fruitful and multiply (that is, have lots of babies), wouldn't the Garden get kind of crowded after a while?

Adam and Eve would have two options. They could stop being so fruitful so that things didn't get too crowded. But then they would be going against God's blessing to be "fruitful and multiply."

Or they could *expand the Garden.*

What if Adam and Eve were always supposed to expand the Garden, making more room for God's living images, making more and more of the world into a house for God's family? It only makes sense. And if it was expected that humanity would expand the Garden, then this is probably what it means for humanity to subdue the earth.

Think about it. Humanity is blessed with the task of blessing all the earth with God's presence. We do this by being God's living images— little statues that represent God's rule in the world. And where God's presence and rule are, there is life and flourishing.

We'll talk more specifically about what this means for each of us later. But we want to end with how God *feels* about entrusting us with this mission of extending his purpose of blessing and flourishing life in the world.

First, God feels great about it. He loves it!

God wants nothing more than to partner with us in his purposes for the world. God loves inviting us into his plans to flourish the world. This is what God does. God longs to gather up the gifts and talents and passions of each one of us and then unfurl us in a whirl of joy and creativity. God delights in working with us, side by side.

Second, God longs to say to us, "Well done! Great job." God is waiting to say this over us, over and over again. Not only does God want to partner with us, but he also longs to rejoice over us—to celebrate us and our work.

Imagine that—being celebrated for doing something significant, something meaningful. We all want this. We all long for it. And that's not a bad thing. God made us to belong in his presence (*God with us*) and to bless the world (*God through us*). And God celebrates when we do both of these.

Practice: Invited

Go back to your joy place one more time. Take time to remember all the details again. Each time you visit this place, it becomes stronger as you create new memories in this place even though you're not physically going there. This time, imagine God with you again. Notice how he enjoys you enjoying this place again. Now imagine that he is inviting you to join him in his family business. What does it feel like to be asked? Talk to him about this.

Reflection

What does it feel like to hear that God delights in working with you?

Recall a time when you finished something big and important. Remember the sense of accomplishment that came with that. Did you want to share that feeling with someone?

Did you want someone to celebrate with you?

Can you imagine God wanting to celebrate his work with you?

Song

Listen to "Fix My Eyes" by For King & Country. How would you live differently if you believed you were part of God's family business?

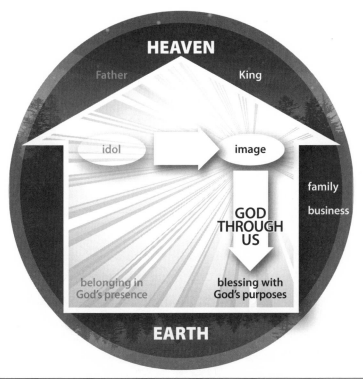

As part of the family business, we bless the world with God's purposes.
As images of the King, we are representatives of his kingdom.

Chapter Five

Does God Really Like Me?

When I (Cyd) was twenty-seven, I lost my mother suddenly to a brain hemorrhage caused by an aneurysm. Just a few short months later, Geoff and I got married and moved to Chicago. Only then did I begin to grieve my mother's death.

My mom and I had our fair share of disagreements, even some all-out battles. Her ideal future for me wasn't always the same one I dreamed of. Her intensely practical advice often felt dream-crushing to me. Her insistence that I check in with her once a week, even as an adult, made me feel like she didn't think I could handle living on my own. She was sometimes skeptical about my choices in life, sometimes concerned, and sometimes disapproving. But she was also my biggest fan. She was always on my side. She loved me, no matter what.

When she was taken from my life so suddenly, her absence became an emotional black hole, sucking my entire life into its gravity. I found myself paralyzed by sorrow and consumed by regret. Even though I was going to leave my job in a month to move to Chicago, I had to quit two weeks sooner than I'd planned because I simply couldn't think or interact with other human beings any more. Getting out of bed in the morning became a monumental task, a mountain I couldn't climb.

The night I gave my notice, I wrote these words in my journal,

Without being able to DO anything, I have no way to measure my worth according to the old standards. I did not realize it until just lately, but I have seen myself in the quality of my work for too many years. I have taken my identity from my job. I have always worked hard and received recognition for my ability to work. Now I have gone from coordinating programs and being responsible for major decisions to having to go to my supervisor and say, "I can't even answer the phone anymore." I am constantly attempting to prove myself "useful and worthy" even by grieving well in order to show that I can do SOMEthing. And so now I see, with more clarity than ever, that I am guilty of measuring my worth by my ability to perform. Now that I cannot perform, what am I worth? This is the question that makes me so vulnerable and desperate to defend myself. Anytime my ability or suggestions are questioned, I am devastated because it is just one more way that I am inadequate.

It's been over twenty years since I wrote that journal entry, and I still struggle with these feelings. You saw that in chapter four when I talked about staying home with a newborn and feeling benched for a season.

These questions of worth and value haunt us all. Divorced from the work we do, the roles we carry, the services we offer, the relationships we have, and the stuff we own, we wonder, *Am I worthy? Am I valuable? What good am I?*

Maybe you don't find significance in your work as much as in your relationships. Maybe you measure your worth by how much people appreciate you and value your place in their life. But what if you can't please someone? What if someone turns away from you and there's nothing you can do to bring them back? You may find yourself wondering, *What's wrong with me? Am I too much? Am I not enough?*

Or maybe you find your security in being able to pay your bills, buy new stuff when you need it, go out for dinner when you want to.

Having the money to create the life you want is what makes you feel like you're on the right track. But when you miss a bill or have to say no to an invitation you can't afford, then what?

Even if you haven't asked yourself these questions recently, chances are good that you have in the past—or you will in the future. These questions of worth, value, and identity have plagued humanity forever. Ever since the fall.

In the last two chapters we've looked at how Adam and Eve were created to live in God's house and to bear God's image, to dwell in the *presence* of God and to extend the *purposes* of God in the world. But it was also in the garden that everything fell apart and caused humanity to forever question who we are and what we are worth.

It is here that humanity lost faith and began to ask, Does God really like me?

The Fall

At the end of Genesis 2 we read that "the man and his wife were both naked, and were not ashamed" (Genesis 2:25). Adam and Eve were totally open and vulnerable with each other and with God. They had nothing to fear and nothing to hide. Humanity belonged in God's presence and was given significant work to do: to bless the world with God's purposes. All was well in the world. They knew they were valued by God. They knew they belonged. They were neither too little nor too much. They were enough. Adam and Eve had a secure foundation of joy in God's presence, from which they could pursue God's purposes.

But that all changed drastically. When we look at the fall of humanity in Genesis chapter three, we often focus on the sin of Adam and Eve. They broke God's law and were guilty because of their actions. And of course the sin and guilt of humanity are very important. But focusing on sin and guilt might make us miss what came before the sin—the thing that created the opportunity for the sin. If you haven't read Genesis 3 in a while, go back and read it again right now.

Here's a broad outline:

- A serpent enters the Garden and asks Eve a question about which fruit Adam and Eve can and can't eat.
- Eve answers that they can eat fruit from any tree but one, which they can't even touch. (Eve actually adds the not touching part to God's command.)
- The serpent then claims that they won't die. Instead, they will become like God, knowing good and evil.
- So Eve takes the fruit and gives some to Adam, and they eat.
- Their eyes are opened: they notice they are naked, they feel guilt, and they feel ashamed. Because of their shame they cover themselves.
- God shows up. Adam and Eve become afraid and hide.
- Because they are hiding, God asks if they have eaten the forbidden fruit. Adam blames Eve. Eve blames the serpent.
- The rest is history.

It all sounds so simple and familiar when outlined like this. But how did Adam and Eve go from being intimately connected with God's presence and his purposes to such devastating separation and shame?

Into Shame

It is true that the fall tells us how sin—and our guilt because of sin— entered the world. But is this the main point of the story? We are told, leading into Genesis 3, that Adam and Eve were naked and un- ashamed (Genesis 2:25). So we are primed to think about how Adam and Eve transitioned from being naked and *unashamed* to covered and *ashamed*. Certainly, sin and guilt before God cause Adam and Eve to be ashamed.

But is there more to the story of shame than this? Is there some- thing we can learn about shame that comes even before sin that might pull us toward sin?

Brené Brown defines shame as "the intensely painful feeling or experience of believing that we are flawed and therefore unworthy of love and belonging—something we've experienced, done, or failed to do makes us unworthy of connection."[1] While guilt is the feeling that *we did* something wrong, shame is the feeling that *we are* something wrong. In his book *The Soul of Shame*, Curt Thompson says, "shame is the emotional feature out of which all that we call sin emerges."[2] Attempting to cover up the feeling that we are bad (shame) causes us to do something that is bad (guilt).

As a relational emotion, shame is the opposite of joy. Joy is being in the presence of someone who is glad to be with you. Shame is fleeing from the presence of someone who is *not* glad to be with you. Joy is the foundation on which we can creatively contribute to the world. Shame creates fear and doubt that we could add anything of value to the world. Joy tells us that we belong and can be a blessing to others. Shame says we are unwelcome and have nothing to offer.

Curt Thompson unpacks the story of the fall with an eye toward how shame starts to work in Adam and Eve. We can summarize Thompson's exploration by saying that shame actually laid the foundation for the first sin. Sin and shame start with *doubt*, grow into emotional *distress*, flower into relational *disintegration*, and end with feelings of *deficiency*—the feeling that something is wrong with me.[3]

Thompson believes, from a neurological perspective, that sin starts from this place of shame. But how does shame start?

The Problem

According to Thompson's perspective, for Adam and Eve shame started with a simple question—"Did God really say?" With this little question the serpent brings shame into the heart and mind of Eve. With that question the serpent tempts Eve to *doubt* herself. Did she hear God right? Is she correctly remembering what he said? Has she made a mistake somewhere? With this tiny bit of self-doubt comes greater doubt about her relationship with God. Maybe she wasn't really paying attention to God. Maybe God meant something different and she misunderstood. Maybe God isn't telling her the whole story. Maybe God is holding out on them. Maybe her relationship with God is not as safe and secure as she thought. In an instant, through one simple question, Eve begins to doubt herself and her relationship to God.

Maybe you can relate to Eve's doubt. Maybe you've doubted your memory of a conversation. You begin to wonder if you heard things right, or you second-guess what the person meant.

From this seed of doubt, *distress* grows in Eve's heart and mind. In her distress, her memory becomes distorted. When she repeats God's command to the serpent, it comes out different from what God said. As Eve becomes insecure in her connection to God, she begins to interpret the conversation with God in a distorted way. In her distress her thoughts become muddled. This cognitive and relational stress is the opportunity for shame to grow.

Have you ever found it hard to think straight when you're stressed out? Have you ever been a little panicked when things don't go according to plan?

The serpent sees Eve's distress and now aims to *disintegrate* her relationship with God. He twists the knife of shame through a lie— "Surely you will not die when you eat the fruit." In Eve's growing state of doubt and distress, this lie confirms Eve's fear that God was holding out on them, that he wasn't telling them the whole truth. Her relationship with God is disintegrating. From doubt to distress to disintegration, shame enters Eve's heart and mind, creating a distance between her and God.

Now that Eve is questioning everything about herself and her relationship with God, now that she feels disconnected and unsure, the serpent goes in for the kill. He offers a way out of the distress. "Eat the fruit. Become like God!" No more distance. No more distress. You'll be equals. You'll know everything. You'll be sure you belong because you'll be just like God.

Not only has the serpent created a relational problem that doesn't actually exist, he has called Eve's very identity into question. The serpent is telling her that she is *deficient*. She is not enough. Through a single question followed by a simple lie the serpent activates shame within Eve. She cannot remember what God said. Her relationship with God is not safe. It's probably her fault, but she's not sure. Now she knows that all of a sudden she is not enough—something is wrong with her, and it needs to be fixed.

Through the introduction of doubt, then distress and a sense of her own deficiency, the serpent was chipping away at the foundation of joy between God and humanity. Eve's identity as an image-bearer of God—all based on the joy of her relationship with God—was being destroyed by shame. This feeling of her disintegrating relationship with God opened the door for sin.

A (False) Solution

Thompson suggests that the first sin began with Eve's perception of a relational problem. Because she chooses to believe the whispers of the serpent, losing confidence in her belonging with God, Eve now feels she needs to add something to her life—the forbidden fruit! This fruit will make her enough. The serpent said so. She must eat the fruit. And so must Adam. Then they won't be deficient anymore, they won't be defective, they won't lack anything—and they won't need to rely on God to get it.

The serpent deceives the images of God by inviting Eve to the dark domain of shame—moving from *doubt* to *distress* to *disintegration* to *deficiency*. And only when he finds her taking the bait and believing she is not fit for God's presence does he offer his solution. Eve believed the lie that her relationship with God was broken, and so she grasped at what the serpent offered.

Eve could have returned to God—returned to the source of joy—in the midst of her distress. She could have turned away from the growing shame caused by her doubts and distress and feelings of deficiency. She could have believed God's goodness and trusted her relationship with him. And by reconnecting with God as her source of identity and purpose she could have defused the bomb of shame growing inside of her. But instead of returning to joy amid shame, she turned further away from God and took the way of sin.

The serpent offered a false solution. The serpent offered a relational shortcut—he offered a *thing*—an object instead of a person. Instead of directing them back toward a relationship with God, the serpent lured Eve toward a shortcut. Eve sees the fruit and thinks it will relieve her distress and deficiency. She thinks it will make her whole again. Eve chooses to act independently. She acts in isolation from others. Eve attempts to protect herself from further relational distress by pursuing an object instead of a person. This object will ask nothing from her while giving her everything. This object will ease her doubts, banish her distress, and fill up her deficiency.

But everything gets much worse after eating the fruit, not better!

What Adam and Eve believed would make them "enough" actually makes them worse off! They go from being naked and unashamed to being exposed and ashamed. They have broken the one rule God asked them to keep. They have sinned against God, turned away from him, and violated their purpose as idols of God. They are so ashamed that they hide from God, afraid he will punish them or turn away from them.

Hiding in Shame

Adam and Eve are guilty and ashamed, so they hide. They fear God will reject them now that they've blown it. Instead of confronting their guilt and shame by pushing back into relationship, they back away from relationship and point fingers. Adam blames Eve. Eve blames the serpent. Everyone runs away, hiding from God, hiding from each other, and hiding from themselves.

And so it goes. Shame first arrives when we fear that a relationship might be broken, that someone we love is not really glad to be with us. Sin comes in the wrong choices we make as we try to inappropriately control those relationships. This sin—and the accompanying guilt—break the relationship further. And then more shame flows as we feel confirmed by the fact that we are unworthy of relationship.

Because of sin, we feel shame. We feel we are not enough—or too much. Everything in us wants to cover it up and hide. Instead of turning to God (or any other person) and rebuilding a foundation for joy, we try to fix it by ourselves. We isolate ourselves, trying to cover our sin, pointing fingers, and hiding from our deficiencies. What seems like a brilliant solution to our sinful choices and feelings of shame ends up driving us further and further into sin and shame, further away from God and away from each other.

And so we think it's easier, even safer to just get away.

Adam and Eve, who had never known neglect or abuse, set the stage for both when they turned away from God and chose to leave God's family. By abandoning the house God made for them—the temple of creation, they abandoned their ability to live as God's images in the world. They decided to leave God's presence and let go of God's purposes in the world. And God respected their decision.

Dried Out Balloons

In the process Adam and Eve lost their capacity to dwell in God's presence and fulfill his purposes.

Think of a balloon. When you pull a balloon out of the package, it is super stretchy. As you blow it up, it seems that it can always hold one more breath. It just keeps getting bigger and bigger. But an old balloon that has been exposed to air for a while (or a whole lot of saliva) loses that stretchiness and will break if you blow it up too much.

Before the fall, Adam and Eve were like enormously stretchy balloons. They were filled with God's breath and wouldn't break. God had "breathed into his (Adam's) nostrils the breath of life" (Genesis 2:7). Humanity was full of the fullness of God's life.

But, separated from God by sin and shame, Adam and Eve became like old, dried-out balloons—tight, unyielding, and rigid—no longer able to hold the full breath of life. Their capacity for God's presence (and ours along with them) was diminished. Sin and shame stole their elasticity. They could no longer handle the fullness of God's presence. It would break them.

So God removed the intensity of his presence by sending Adam and Eve away. They could no longer believe or receive God's love and joy. They had become disconnected from God. And so God had to tie off the balloon and let them float away for a time.

Leaving God's Family

God won't force us into his family. He won't force us to remain in his presence. He won't force us to pursue his purposes. And if we insist on leaving, God won't force us to stay.

Adam and Eve chose to leave God's house. As a good Father, God's heart broke. But as a loving Father, he let them go. The intensity of Adam and Eve's sin and shame wouldn't allow them to live within the intensity of God's love. It would overwhelm them.

They needed more space. Not because God was abandoning humanity or was sick of them. They needed more space because by disconnecting from God—who is the source of all life—all of humanity became weak and brittle. Humanity walked away from the path of life and entered into the slow, suffocating realm of death: spiritually, relationally, and physically. By sending them away from his presence, God was respecting their choice.

God's decision to do this had nothing to do with anger, hate, disgust, or disappointment. Sure, Adam and Eve probably felt like God was angry and disappointed with them. They probably felt that God didn't even like them anymore.

But God removed his presence as an act of love and mercy.

God didn't want them to be utterly destroyed. God didn't want humanity to be lost forever. His mercy allowed their old and rigid balloon skin to remain intact by giving them safe distance from his living breath. If he had not stopped breathing his fullness into them, they would have been destroyed.

When Adam and Eve lost God's presence, they also lost God's purposes for their lives. They were supposed to be a conduit of God's blessing in the world. Through humanity the world would receive God's kingdom and flourish in his life. But now, in their shame, they lost access to God and the ability to bless the world.

This is the story of how sin spiraled into shame, producing more sin, causing more shame, and on and on. If only Adam and Eve had allowed the shame of disconnection to drive them back to the relationship, they could have sought restoration.

Loss of Presence and Purpose

When I (Cyd) experienced disconnection from my mom, I realized just how much her presence had meant in my life. I still longed for her blessing. I wanted her to see me, to know me—not just as her daughter but as a woman who had something to contribute to the world. Her voice had become my magnetic north, and I had found my direction by alternating between aligning with her and resisting her pull. When she was suddenly gone, I was completely disoriented. My sense of who I was and what I was doing was destroyed by her absence.

Likewise, the death caused by Adam and Eve made all of us lose our way. God didn't die; we did. Our sin and shame sucked the life right out of us. And now, in the absence of God's presence, we don't know who to be or what to do.

And so we doubt: *Am I enough? Am I worthy? Does God see me? Does God like me?* And as we wrestle with those doubts, we fall into distress. We believe we are defective: either too much or not enough. And feeling defective, we begin to believe that God couldn't possibly want to be with us. In our shame we distance ourselves from God, preferring the absence of God to the outright rejection of God. We reject God before God can reject us.

This is the spiral of sin and shame we've all inherited.

Doubt, distress, deficiency, and distance are the background of our lives. We seek to cover up the pain and the death that came from losing God's presence and purposes. The spiral of sin and shame is as powerful today as it was for Adam and Eve.

But don't lose hope. God didn't give up after the Garden. He wasn't content to allow this separation to become the status quo. He is not finished yet!

Practice: Returning to Joy

Now that you've visited your joy place several times, we hope you can see how you can return to that place at any time and under any circumstances. Each time you come home to your joy place, good things happen in your brain. You're building capacity. You're creating more room for joy. The most important time to return to your joy place is when you feel the shame and disconnection of Eve when the serpent questioned her about God's command. Rather than trying to hide your shame or manage your sin, you can return to your place of joy. You can remember all the sights, sounds, tastes, feels, and smells. You can remember that God is there.

And in that place, he can remind you of his desire to be with you, reconnect with you, and return you to joy. In that place you can talk to him about your doubts, shame, and sins. And he can reassure you of your belonging in his presence and his desire to continue to invite you into his work. In this place you can return to joy as you connect with God.

Reflection

In what ways do you find yourself trying to take relational shortcuts?

What might change if you went to God in those places instead of looking for solutions?

Song

As you listen to "Broken Things" by Matthew West, ask if you've felt unworthy to be in God's presence.

Because humanity chose the way of death, God's house of joy is destroyed. Heaven and earth can no longer overlap, and humanity loses God's presence and purposes.

Part Two

God's House

Chapter Six

Why Do I Have to Wait?

*I*n summer 2000 we moved from Santa Cruz, California, to Chicago, Illinois. You might ask why we would ever leave the ocean, the mountains, and the forests of Northern California. Good question.

I (Geoff) always knew I would go to seminary after college. The question was where. The options were between a well-known seminary in Southern California and a well-known seminary in Chicago. Cyd's family was in Grand Rapids, Michigan, a couple of hours from Chicago. Cyd's mom had died suddenly a few months before we were married. And because her mom had been the hub of the wheel in her family, we thought it would be good for Cyd to be near her family as they reorganized after her mom's death.

So we packed up our Subaru hatchback with everything we owned and drove over the mountains and across the plains to Chicago.

It was quite disorienting for me. We exchanged the Pacific Ocean for Lake Michigan, mighty mountains for endless plains, beach weather for bitter winters. I was attending a new school, Cyd was working a new job, and we needed to find a new church.

We were disoriented and drifting during our first year in Chicago— and Cyd was only just starting to grieve the death of her mother. Our first year of marriage was supposed to be joyful bliss. Instead, it was full of grief and doubts.

Where Did God Go?

All of us have gone through seasons like this, moving from what we know and past our comfort zones. Sometimes we choose this change when we go to school or change jobs. Sometimes it's forced on us— like when we're let go from a job, our health takes a turn for the worse, or we lose a loved one unexpectedly.

Maybe we've wandered away from where we should be. Maybe we made the wrong choice, turned down the wrong path. Or maybe it feels like God is the one who wandered. When we go to the places where we are accustomed to finding God, he doesn't seem to be there.

Where did God go? Where did we go? How did we get here? If God built a home for us to be in together, why is he so hard to find? We feel like we're wandering, waiting for God to show up, feeling unwanted because he doesn't seem to want to be with us.

Wandering . . . waiting . . . unwanted.

The truth is, after the fall of the human race we have moments when we feel like this. We all miss the joy of God's presence and lack the desire to pursue his purposes. Sometimes we feel like we don't belong and that we have nothing to bless others with.

But as we'll see, God doesn't abandoned those who wander, wait, and feel unwanted—in fact, he's with them in a special way. And God is still using those people—the ones who don't seem to belong—to bring his blessing to the world.

End of the Line

To understand how God is with the wandering, the waiting, and the unwanted, we need to pick up the story of God's work in the world after the fall.

Where is God's presence to be found after the fall? What will become of God's blessing on and through humanity? If people belong in God's presence, what will happen now that God has removed his presence? Will they ever be together again? Will heaven and earth ever overlap again?

These questions haunt us when we finish Genesis 1–11. When we get to the end of Genesis 11, it's as if humanity has reached the end of the line. Time for everyone to get off. And the name of the last station? Death!

We see a snapshot of this death at the end of Genesis 11 as the story zooms in on one man's family. A man named Terah has three sons. One of them dies before Terah does—for a parent to bury a child is a tragedy in any time or place. Another son marries, and then we hear nothing more about him. It's like he disappears. And Terah's third son, Abraham, marries Sarah—but she is barren.[1] Then Terah dies.

The death of a son. The disappearance of a son. Then the death of a father with no heirs to carry on the family name. The line of Terah seems to end in the bitter barrenness of Sarah.

The blessing of God to humanity—to be fruitful and multiply, to fill the earth—seems to end in barrenness and death. It's the end of the line for Terah's family. And the tragedy of this one family represents the death that has come to all families because of the fall.

Without God's life-giving presence there is only death. Without God's blessing there is only the curse of death. Without heaven and earth overlapping—there is only death.

And we all have moments when the fall seems to overcome any goodness in our lives—moments that feel like the end of the line, a dead end. The doors of hope have all closed, the winds of change have died down, and the fires of passion have all gone out.

Blessing from Barrenness

But out of the death-dealing destruction of sin comes the life-giving blessing of God.

This is the shift as we move from Genesis 11 to Genesis 12. Over the stale ashes of death, a fresh wind is blowing. Life is coming again. God is going to show his people the way home again. This way is not back to how things were in the Garden. God is going to build a new home! But first, God needs to call a new family.

Seemingly out of nowhere, God calls Abraham—and his call is loaded with goodness and promise. God tells Abraham:

> Go from your country and your kindred and your father's house to the land that I will show you. I will make of you a great nation, and I will bless you, and make your name great, so that you will be a blessing. I will bless those who bless you, and the one who curses you I will curse; and in you all the families of the earth shall be blessed. (Genesis 12:1-3)

These verses are pregnant with meaning and hope. To get at that hope, we need to ask some questions: Who? Why? and Where?

Who does God call? We have to remember that Sarah is barren, without hope of children. Being barren was the greatest shame for a woman in ancient cultures and in the context of the Genesis story a sign of the curse. But God promises to bring blessing through a family that has no future, no hope, and no life. God starts at the dead end, the end of the line. God plants a seed of blessing right where death reigned.

Why does God call Abraham? God calls Abraham for a few reasons. First, he wants to fulfill Abraham's longing for a son. He wants Abraham to be fruitful, to multiply—just like the blessing God gave Adam and Eve. Second, God wants to bring blessing to the whole world—to all the families of the earth! God is going to open the spigot of blessing to humanity through a family that is not even a family yet. The blessing God gave to Adam and Eve—to be fruitful and multiply, to fill the earth—is now promised to flow through a barren family. That's quite the plot twist. In fact, God promises to make Abraham fruitful (Genesis 17:6) and his son Isaac's descendants as many as the stars (Genesis 26:4, 24), showing that God is bestowing the blessing promised to Adam and Eve on Abraham's family.

Where does God call Abraham to go? This is the tricky part. God tells Abraham to go to a land that God will show him. God is asking Abraham and Sarah to leave their land, their families—the place where they belong—and to trust him as he leads them who knows where.

When we left California, we at least knew we were going to Chicago. We already had an apartment picked out. We already had a school to attend. It was a hard transition, but everything wasn't up for grabs. The second time we moved, after we'd lived in that house for fifteen years, was much more difficult. Not only had we accumulated a lot of stuff but we'd developed many meaningful connections too. We were firmly planted, well-rooted, and established in a community we loved.

Leaving Chicago with our two kids to go to Grand Rapids was significantly harder than leaving California had been, but even so, we knew where we were going before we left. We were called by a church, welcomed by new friends and Cyd's sister and Dad. But Abraham and Sarah set out with nothing like that: no destination, no assurances, nothing.

God may be about to do something in your lifeless place, and it might not look like anything you've seen before. God brings blessing out of barrenness. But we often have to wait much longer than we would expect or hope. If God started at a dead end to save humanity, then surely God can bring forth blessing from the barren places in your life as well. But waiting for it is tough!

Waiting and Waiting

Our older son, Soren, had a lesson in waiting in the spring of his thirteenth year. He wanted to make some money, so he got a job as a baseball umpire. He went to training and learned how to make calls with authority and tenacity. He picked up his uniform and showed up for his first game.

But there was no game. I (Cyd) had put it on the calendar for the wrong week. On the correct day he showed up to umpire his first game. This time, it rained. The game was canceled. The next week, he finally umpired a couple of games.

Now he had to wait for the promised paycheck. He went to the mailbox daily, expecting that check. Daily, he was disappointed. After two weeks of waiting for the check to arrive in the mailbox, it finally came. He had his own student checking account with a mobile app, and he enthusiastically photographed the check to deposit to his account. But the balance in his account didn't immediately increase after depositing the check. We explained that it can take a full business day for the account to update when you make a deposit. All he heard was "More waiting!"

For the rest of that afternoon and evening, he checked the balance every few minutes on his app, frustrated that it hadn't yet appeared. When would it show up? A whole month after beginning this job with the hope of making some money, he still didn't have anything to show for it.

He almost lost his mind waiting for that paycheck!

Waiting and Wandering

Abraham was seventy years old when God promised to bring him to a new home, a new land. Ten years later, God reminded Abraham that he would be the father of a great nation. Abraham promptly reminded God that he still had no children! Almost fifteen years after that, God visited Abraham again—when Abraham was ninety-nine years old— to reiterate his promise by changing their names from Abram to Abraham and Sarai to Sarah.[2] And again, Abraham mentions that he and Sarah still have no children (Genesis 12:1-4; 15:1-21; 16:3; 17:1-22).

So, what is God doing? Why do Abraham and Sarah have to wait so long for the promise to be fulfilled?

Not only are they waiting for the promised child, they're also wandering around the Promised Land. God promised the land of Canaan to Abraham and his descendants, but for the rest of their lives they were just nomads, wandering from place to place and trying to stay out of trouble with the locals.

What is God doing? Why take so long to fulfill the promises? How is this leading up to the new home he is making for his people to live with him? Why does God work so slowly?

If God wanted to restart his blessing in the world and wanted to make sure everyone knew about it, wouldn't it make sense to launch with a big event? Something to catch everyone's attention? Something no one could deny?

But God didn't do any of this. Instead, God made a promise to one, single family. Only one! And then they wait and they wander for twenty-five years! Seems like a missed opportunity.

God's Strategy

To understand why God uses waiting and wandering, we need to remember what Adam and Eve turned their backs on—and what all of us refuse almost every day in our sin and shame. Adam and Eve abandoned their purpose to live as God's image in the world. They abandoned their place in God's presence. And they abandoned their partnership in God's purpose for the whole world.

They exchanged their God-given home to wander the world without God. They traded all the resources God had given them for the false power of pretending to be gods and attempting to rule over others.

In this world after the fall, those with power never wait. They take what they want when they want it. In this world after the fall, those with power never wander. They go where they want as if they own the place. The people with the most power, influence, or wealth don't have to wait or wander. Their time is much too valuable and their destination is too important.

But God knows that getting what you want when you want it is not real power. Real power is being able to rest in the presence of God and to work toward his purposes in the world. To show everyone this kind of power, God needs to unmask and undermine the false powers that currently rule the world. To do this he needs to show us just how dead the dead end really is.

Throughout the Bible and through history God makes his home with unlikely people, with those who don't seem to belong, with people who don't seem important. These are the same people he invites to join him in the family business of bringing blessing to the whole world. God called Abraham and Sarah and put them through rigorous training in waiting and wandering. He did this to show the world that true blessing—and true power—comes to and through those who wait and wander.

But even through their times of waiting and wandering God was always with them. No matter how much they wandered, God was with them. They were home with God. Even though they waited for the promised child and they wandered the Promised Land, God was always near them and blessing them. In fact, Abraham and Sarah grew wealthy and powerful because God watched over them in their waiting and wandering.

And God's blessing is not just for those who wait and wander. It comes even to the unwanted.

God Sees the Unwanted

Behind Abraham and Sarah's story of waiting and wandering is another story, the story of an unwanted slave named Hagar (Genesis 16:1-16; 21:8-21).

Like many of us would, Abraham and Sarah began to wonder if faithfulness might not look like getting more involved in making sure the promise happened. This is where Hagar comes in. By no choice of her own, Hagar comes into the household of Abraham and Sarah as a slave. She is not wanted for who she is as a person but only because she is useful. Confused about God's timeline, Sarah decides to help by having Hagar act as a surrogate mother and bear a child for Abraham. Hagar is only a means to an end.

But as soon as Hagar becomes pregnant, Sarah's hope becomes hatred. She can't stand the sight of Hagar. Sarah becomes so cruel to Hagar that Hagar flees into the wilderness—presumably to die.

In the wilderness, unwanted and unloved, God finds her. In her distress God comes to her to be with her. He sees her, hears her, understands her, and is glad to be with her. He speaks to Hagar and invites her to speak to him. He tells her that he wants to be with her, the unwanted one, and that he will bless her. God is building a foundation of empathy, the foundation of a connected relationship, with Hagar. Through attuning to her, God is rebuilding the possibility for joy, a joy that gives Hagar the courage to return to Abraham (Genesis 16:1-16).

Things get better for a season. Hagar's son is born and is named Ishmael. God promises to bless him and make him into a great nation. But then Sarah finally gives birth to Isaac, the promised child of God, and Sarah asks Abraham to banish Hagar and Ishmael. Sarah doesn't want her son Isaac to share his inheritance with the son of a slave. So Hagar again finds herself unwanted and driven into the wilderness. She and her son are so close to death that Hagar walks away so she doesn't have to watch Ishmael die.

But once again God sees Hagar. He sees Ishmael. He hears them crying, and he comes to them. They had been banished from the household of Abraham, but God went to find them. He not only provides water for their physical needs but meets their emotional and spiritual craving. Through Hagar, an unwanted outsider, God reveals himself as the one who sees, the one who cares deeply about each of his children, the one who desires that no one would be without a home or a family.

Seen and Heard by God

Maybe as you read this you find yourself resonating with Hagar's story. Maybe you've been mistreated. Maybe you've had to run away from a bad situation. Maybe you voluntarily left a good situation and would do anything to get it back, but you can't. Maybe you feel lost, weak, wandering, or unwanted. Maybe there's no one in your life who seems to see, hear, and understand you. Maybe no one is glad to be with you.

But God won't give up on you. He is glad to be with you. No matter what you have done, no matter what you've walked away from, no matter how unseen you might feel, how misunderstood, or how unwanted, God is coming to you. God is coming to you in your weak, wandering, and unwanted places. He understands how you got there, and instead of passing judgment on you he meets you right where you are. He comes to you in your wilderness and is with you. He comes, bringing living water and speaking words of hope.

You are wanted. You belong. And you have a purpose. God is not done yet. This dead end is not the end. God is still inviting you to come along, to be a blessing.

Through Abraham and Sarah, God is beginning to build a new home for his people—a place where he can be present to them. He's also planning to bless the whole world through this home, to flourish life everywhere. Adam and Eve may have chosen to turn away from God's home and to neglect God's work, but God has not given up.

Practice: Immanuel Journaling, Part 1

- Begin with gratitude. What things—both big and small—can you thank God for today? How does he respond to your gratitude? What might he say to you about that?
- What does God see when he looks at you today? Let him speak in the first person: "I see you sitting in your favorite chair, wearing . . ."

- What does God hear when he listens to your thoughts? "I hear you wondering about . . . worrying about . . . excited about . . . frustrated about . . ."
- What does it feel like to remember that God meets you where you are, seeing you and hearing your thoughts and feelings?[3]

Reflection

How often do you let God meet you where you really are?

Do you feel the need to get somewhere or do something before you feel like you can meet with God?

Or can you, like Hagar, allow God to come to you wherever you are—not where you think you should be or wish you could be?

Song

While listening to "God Only Knows" by For King & Country, ask if you really believe that God sees and knows all you are going through.

Through Abraham's family, God will rebuild a place for heaven and earth to overlap again.

Chapter Seven

Is God Angry with Me?

When our sons were young, I (Cyd) was enjoying a pleasant shopping trip to Trader Joe's with the kids. It was one of those moments when I felt especially connected to them. They were enjoying me and each other, and I was enjoying them.

While I was comparing ingredients, I noticed a store employee giving me an inquisitive look and pointing at my four-year-old son, as if to say, "Does he belong to you?" This couldn't be good. Everything in me wanted to run away.

Being a responsible grown-up I didn't run away. I went over to the man in the Hawaiian shirt and found out what had happened. My curious son had been enjoying the result of pushing his fingers over the plastic wrapping on a ready-to-bake pizza, and now the cheese had squished together into the center of the pizza. The employee said, "I just wanted to make sure you knew what your son was up to."

No. I guess I hadn't known. Cue the bad parent shame soundtrack. Sheepishly, I offered to buy the damaged pizza, but with a flip of his hand the man said it was okay.

No. It was not okay. I was ashamed, embarrassed. I wanted to hide. I'd been called out as a bad parent. I was turning in on myself.

From a faraway place, I heard my son whimpering, "I'm so sorry, I'm so sorry, I'm so sorry," but I was more focused on saving face in public than on staying connected with him. I told him there would be a consequence and that he would need to wait until we got into the car to talk about it. There was still shopping to do. I'm far too practical to leave a store without finishing my list.

My little boy tried to crawl into his shirt like a turtle. He was miserable, trying not to cry, scanning the store madly, hoping to avoid the evil man in the festive shirt. I was focused on myself, determined to save face and finish my list without another incident. As we walked across the parking lot, he blurted, "I never want to go to Trader Joe's again! I hate that place!"

Suddenly it dawned on me. Alone in my own shame, I had left him alone in his shame. We were both doing the same thing—running from our shame. It's like we were standing again in the Garden, naked and exposed, desperately looking for a way to disappear.

Feeling Exposed

We've all been there. We observe something awful in ourselves or someone points it out. We feel exposed, undone. We want to run away and hide or fight back or just freeze like a rabbit in the presence of a wolf. And when we're in this place, we turn inward like turtles to protect ourselves from further pain. Or we attack like tigers, hurling ourselves against the threat. In either case, if we're not careful, we can find ourselves hating ourselves, the other person, and even the particular place that triggered the feelings of shame.

Shame is the opposite of joy. It is the experience of disconnection—it feels wrong to be in the presence of someone else. Our cheeks burn and our palms sweat. We find ourselves afraid to be in the presence of that person again.

But does that mean the person we're disconnected from is against us? That their presence is really so dangerous? Is it them, or is it us?

Fiery Sun

One summer we took the boys on a family trip to California to explore where I (Geoff) grew up. We spent a couple of days on the northern end of Monterey Bay in Santa Cruz.

Santa Cruz is a huge surfing town. Wetsuits—suits made of neoprene fabric that trap a small layer of water between the skin and the suit—were first manufactured in Santa Cruz by the iconic Jack O'Neill to allow surfers to last longer in the cold waters of the Pacific. So when we took the boys surfing, we rented wetsuits to keep us warm all day.

It was glorious. We were in and out of the water for about eight hours, learning to read the sets, paddling into the bowl of the wave, and then popping up and riding the wave to the shore. And because we had wetsuits covering us from wrist to ankle, we never needed to reapply sunscreen.

It was a joy to share our love of surfing with our kids. We delighted as they caught their first waves, hooting and hollering and celebrating their success. And they were euphoric as they paddled around, sat on their boards, and rode wave after wave. It was one of those perfect family days that will live in our memories forever. We were so connected and so joyful to be together!

Except we had overlooked one thing.

At the end of the day the backs of our hands and the tops of our feet were sunburned, and both of our kids had second-degree burn blisters on their ears. We had worn wetsuits and considered ourselves safe from the sun, but we forgot to protect the exposed parts of our pasty, Dutch-German skin.

That night, as we lay in bed in the hotel, we were all miserable. We couldn't get comfortable. Every time the sheets scraped across the tender parts of skin or someone rolled onto an ear there would be yelps of pain, exclamations of frustration, and even some tears. We snapped at each other. We made accusations about whose fault it was. We alternated between turtles and tigers.

The trauma of the sunburn was overshadowing the joy of the day. All the goodness of our day at the beach was lost as we fixated on our sunburned extremities and who or what we could blame.

The same thing can happen in our relationship with God. All the joy can evaporate in a moment when we feel threatened or in pain.

We see this in the story of the exodus when God delivered Israel from slavery so that he might dwell in their presence forever.

Flourishing People?

At the end of the book of Genesis God raises up Joseph (Abraham's great-grandson) to save his people from famine by moving Abraham's descendants to Egypt. There, they flourished for generations. God was keeping his promise to Abraham that his children would be fruitful and multiply, and that they would be a blessing to all nations.

But pharaoh—the king of Egypt—resisted God's blessing on and through the Israelites and enslaved them. Everything was going horribly wrong for God's chosen people. So God decided to do something about it.

He visits Moses—who was himself wandering and unwanted (notice a pattern?) and tells Moses that he is the God of his fathers—the God of Abraham, Isaac, and Jacob. God reminds Moses of the family he belongs to. And then God speaks the words of a loving Father, deeply concerned about his children. He tells Moses, "I have observed the misery of my people . . . I have heard their cry . . . I know their sufferings" (Exodus 3:7).

God isn't distant and aloof, concerned only about his plan. He sees, hears, and understands the plight of his children. God—as a good Father—even calls Israel his firstborn son (Exodus 4:22).

And that's not all! God is going to act. "I have come down to deliver them from the Egyptians, and to bring them up out of that land to a good and broad land, a land flowing with milk and honey" (Exodus 3:8). God doesn't just understand what his children are suffering; he's going to do something about it! He's going to deliver them!

Pharaoh, a man of power (someone who has never had to wait or wander or deal with being unwanted), is threatened by God's man Moses. And so pharaoh brings out the tiger of resistance and attacks (just like many of us do). Pharaoh takes out his anger on the Israelites, God's firstborn, and he persecutes them even more. When God makes it clear through the ten plagues that he's not leaving without Israel, pharaoh finally relents.

God fulfills his promise to Israel! He sees their misery, he hears their cries, he knows their sufferings, and he comes down and delivers them! But this deliverance isn't even the main point, as we will see soon. The main point is dwelling—God *with* us.

A Fiery God

But if God wants to be with Israel—ultimately, to be with all of us— why is he so scary sometimes? Why does God seem so angry in the Bible?

We don't want to be selective in our reading of the Bible. In the same chapter where God expresses his special love and devotion to Israel (Exodus 19), he also shows up as a fiery storm of smoke, thunder, and lightning, telling the people not to approach Mount Sinai lest they die.

What's up with that? Is God a schizophrenic Father who turns on a dime from tender to terrible?

If God's deliverance of Israel is so that God can be with his people, why all the threats? If God's presence brings blessing to Israel, why the burning mountain? How do we fit this terrifying God with the earlier image of God as a loving Father rescuing and providing for his children?

Is God's presence going to bless Israel, or will it burn them up?

Think back to our story about getting sunburned while surfing. Was the sun evil, angry, or mean when we were sunburned? Did the sun hate us? No. The problem is that we—as pale-skinned Midwesterners— were not prepared to stand unprotected in its presence all day. Just because our skin felt punished by the sun doesn't mean the sun was mean, angry, or threatening.

In the same way Israel—and in fact, all of humanity—is unable to stand unprotected in God's presence. God desires nothing more than to be with us and bless us, but he also knows we are not prepared to live fully in his presence. All of humanity—like Israel—is tainted by sin. And sin (as we saw in chap. 5) destroys our capacity to dwell in God's presence.

The Terror Is Real

Let's go back to the Trader Joe's incident for a moment. My son was terrified of an employee who was simply pointing out that it's not okay to damage the pizzas. Nobody wants to buy a pizza that has been massaged by the fingers of a four-year-old. The employee wasn't evil, he was being informative. But the terror for my son was real. And the shame for me was real.

Because of sin, we all have a deep sense that we're not okay. We know there is something deeply flawed about us. And anything—no matter how small—can confirm those feelings. At Sinai, in the presence of a smoking, thundering, burning mountain, the Israelites were acutely aware of their flaws, and they were terrified. There's a reason why angels always greet people with the words, "Do not be afraid." The full and glorious presence of the God of the universe is terrifying.

But does that mean that God is terrible?

A Fireplace

Many of us have fond memories of staring into a fireplace—it's so mesmerizing, so calming. We like having fireplaces in our houses or apartments, but we don't really need them. Most of us have other ways to heat our homes and cook our food.

But in the past, a wood-burning fireplace or stove was essential for life, especially in colder climates. The fireplace was not only the source of warmth but also the place for cooking meals. Everyone in the house received the blessing of warmth and food through the fireplace.

But if the fire got out of the fireplace, what would happen? The whole house would burn down. Fire is a blessing in one context but a threat in another.

It is the same with God's presence. God wants to be with us. He wants his people to dwell in his presence again. And his presence (his glory) is the source of warmth and nourishment. But because of sin, God's presence also has the potential to burn down the entire house of humanity.

This is the dilemma the Israelites experienced at Mount Sinai: How can the fiery presence of God be safe enough for Israel so that they can receive the blessing of God's presence? This is the question God answered on Mount Sinai. God didn't just give the Ten Commandments to Moses on the mountain. He also gave him the building plans for a fireplace for his glory—a new house—so that God could "dwell among them"—so that God's presence could bless them without burning them (Exodus 25:8).

This fireplace for God's glory is called the tabernacle; later it was the temple. About the tabernacle, God said, "I will meet with the Israelites there, and it shall be sanctified by my glory . . . I will dwell among the Israelites, and I will be their God. And they shall know that I am the LORD their God, who brought them out of the land of Egypt that I might dwell among them" (Exodus 29:43, 45-56).

You can't get much clearer than that. God's deliverance was for dwelling so God's presence could overflow in blessing for Israel—and eventually for all humanity.

Just like our family wasn't able to withstand the California sun, Israel—like all of sinful humanity—wasn't capable of living in God's presence unprotected. And so God made a way (first the tabernacle and then the temple) for his people to be warmed and nourished in his presence without being destroyed.

This is the promise of *God with us.*

Heaven and Earth Overlapping

Earlier we talked about how all creation was supposed to be filled with God's glory, how "the heavens are telling the glory of God" and "the whole earth is full of his glory" (Psalm 19:1; Isaiah 6:3). Heaven (the place of God) and earth (the place of humanity) were supposed to fully overlap one another. All this was lost in the fall, as heaven and earth were torn apart.

But now—at the end of the book of Exodus—God's presence returns to humanity! Heaven and earth are coming together through the tabernacle. Not content to be separated from his people, God has now made a way to dwell with humanity again. Beginning with Abraham and Sarah, and continuing with Israel, God is reuniting heaven and earth.

And with this reunion comes the sense of a return home—and with a return home comes the return of joy. In God's presence Israel was able to return to joy and to the security of a trusting relationship.

In the beginning creation responded to the overlapping of heaven and earth with great joy. In God's presence there is the fullness of joy. Now that God's presence has returned to the earth in the tabernacle, it makes sense that the psalms—the worship songs of the Israelites—would be filled with songs of joy. The people go up to the tabernacle with joy. Why? Because that is where the presence of God is found (Psalm 5:11; 16:11; 47; 68:3; 122; 126; 128; 132; 134; Isaiah 35:1-10).

Returning Home

One of my (Cyd's) favorite things about coming home to my family after I've been away for a night or two is the exuberant hug I receive from one of our sons. When he sees me home again, his face breaks into a huge grin, his pace quickens, and he comes straight to me for a hug before I've even taken the bags off my shoulders. We both sigh, relaxing into the familiarity of the embrace. He's glad to be with me again. I'm glad to be with him again. We are both filled with joy.

Israel can now approach the presence of God with this kind of joy and exuberance in the tabernacle/temple. And God experiences this kind of delight as he is able to once again enjoy the fellowship of his children.

God and humanity are together again in this special place of reunion. Heaven and earth come together in the tabernacle/temple. And where heaven and earth overlap, humanity can again live as the image of God—both as God's dwelling place and as the extension of God's blessing in the world.

Returning to Joy

At Trader Joe's, after my son said he never wanted to go there again, my heart broke. I realized how disconnected he felt from me, and how he projected all the hurt onto the place we were—Trader Joe's. My own embarrassment at his behavior was only a tiny glimmer of the shame and despair he was experiencing. Being only four, he probably wondered if anything would ever be okay again. I realized that the withdrawal of my (emotional) presence had made everything so much worse for him.

In the middle of the parking lot, I knelt down next to him and looked him in the eye. I drew near to him. "I love you. I'm so glad you're my son." He leaped into my arms and sobbed. We were together again. Everything was going to be all right. We were both able to return to joy through connection.

God doesn't withhold his presence from us. He's not a stern parent who lets us stew in our shame like I did that day. Instead, our Father sees, hears, and understands our troubles—and what's more, he does something about them. He makes a way to come down and draw near. He overcomes our incapacity to dwell in his presence so we can live in relationship with him again. God comes so that we can return to joy.

Practice: Immanuel Journaling, Part 2

Repeat part 1 from chapter six (gratitude, I see, I hear), then add:

- What does God understand about what he's seeing and hearing? "I understand how big this is . . . I know how long you've been waiting . . . I understand how you got here . . . I get it. I know."
- Let God express his joy in being with you, right here and right now where you are. "I'm glad to be with you in this."
- How might God be *for* you in this? How might he want to make your life flourish and bless the people in your life? "I'm doing something here . . . I'm making all things new . . . I'm flourishing your life by . . ."[1]

Reflection

Think back to a time when you experienced shame and you chose to allow someone who loves you to see it, to be with you in it. How was it different to be with someone who loved you rather than to be alone and isolated?

If you've never allowed someone to be with you when you're experiencing shame, what do you think it would be like to allow God to be with you?

What might it be like to try to recognize his presence with you in that moment and in that place.

Song

As you listen to "If We're Honest" by Francesca Battistelli, reflect on just how hard it is to be open and vulnerable with others.

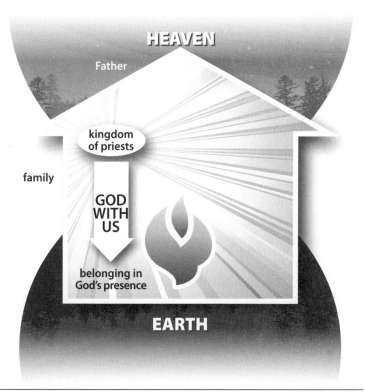

As God makes Israel a kingdom of priests, his presence fills the
tabernacle like a fire filling a fireplace.

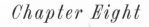

Chapter Eight

Is God Disappointed with Me?

*D*o you ever feel like nothing you do is ever good enough? That you need to be perfect, otherwise why bother?

I (Cyd) started playing the clarinet when I was in the fifth grade. My band director encouraged me to start taking private lessons, which I did. My teacher was a wonderful man who knew the balance between encouraging warmth and challenging firmness. He was humble, genuine, and down-to-earth, but he knew how to inspire me to live into the music and play my heart out. I fell in love with the clarinet and decided to make it my career.

When I went to a prestigious summer music camp, I was exposed to a new teacher. She was terrifying. I had always practiced (although not as much as I could have), but this woman was unappeasable. Every time I walked into a lesson feeling proud of my progress or excited to prove I could play a difficult passage, she let me know exactly how I had failed. I would walk out nearly in tears. Whatever I played was never good enough. Nothing short of perfection was good enough for her. I internalized her need for perfection and began to practice relentlessly, using the "penny method."

In order to get the difficult passages "into my fingers," I would put a stack of ten pennies on the music stand. I began by playing the passage as slowly as I needed to in order to play it perfectly. As soon as I could play it flawlessly once, I moved one penny to the other side of the stand. I repeated it. If it was perfect again, I moved a second penny. As long as I continued to play the passage without mistakes, I could move pennies to the other side. When I reached all ten, I bumped up the metronome speed and started again with all ten pennies on the left side. However, if I made a single mistake—even if it was the ninth time through, I moved all the pennies back to the left side and started over. It was a punishing process—but it brought me closer to perfection. This habit stayed with me into college as I continued to pursue a career in music performance.

But something happened on my way to perfection.

I lost my love for music. It had become about perfection, not passion. It was about pleasing the unappeasable teacher, not enjoying the music. I lived in fear of being criticized for getting it wrong, not in anticipation of the beauty and joy of playing. The music had died for me.

Is God Disgusted with Me?

I hadn't realized that I experienced God the same way I experienced that clarinet teacher. It felt like nothing was ever good enough for God. I felt that God was always displeased with anything less than perfection. Whenever I went to him for encouragement or affirmation, I heard, "Okay, but what you really need to do is . . ."

Often, when we read the Bible, we are confronted with our failing, our inability to reach the high bar set for us. Maybe we imagine God looking at us with disappointment and frustration. We imagine him pointing out our mistakes, our failures, and in response we resolve to work harder, to do better. We go through our days with our penny stacks, trying to do the right things, say the right words, feel the right ways. And every time we fail, we become acutely aware—yet again—of just how short we fall. We move our pennies back to the left and get back to work, hoping to do better, but every time we lose more hope of ever pleasing the impossibly perfect God—the God who is holy.

There have been seasons in my life when I have been so aware of my failures that I didn't even want to spend time in Scripture or in prayer. I was sure that God must be irritated with me, frustrated by my lack of resolve, disappointed with my inability to obey, disgusted with me. It was better to avoid his presence altogether than to be confronted with my failure.

During those seasons my love for God was nearly dead. There was no joy in trying to appease an unappeasable taskmaster. I had no joy in being in God's presence because I imagined God was disgusted with me—because God was holy, and I was not. And if God is holy and I am not, then God has no joy for me, no love for me—and he certainly doesn't like me.

Impossible Holiness

When we consider God's holiness, we might look at God's perfect standard and know, deep down, that it's impossible for us to meet it. We might try to steer clear of anything that might stain us, avoiding certain movies, social gatherings, anything of questionable influence. We try to focus on whatever is pure and pleasing to God (Philippians 4:8).

But no matter how hard we try, we keep failing—"falling short" (Romans 3:23). Everyone falls short. Everyone misses the mark. And so we become hopeless. Why bother? Nothing we ever do will be good enough.

We've already seen in chapter seven that God's primary concern is being with us. But it's easy to think God actually cares most about perfection. After all, God does say to Israel, "Be holy, for I am holy" (Leviticus 11:44-45; 19:2; 20:7, 26).

This call to holiness is confusing—and condemning—because we often misunderstand what it means. We often think that to be holy means to be "set apart"—to be pure, clean, unstained. We think this means we should look, talk, and act differently from others, to be separate. And when we don't, we should feel ashamed, like Adam and Eve did.

But being set apart is only part of the story of holiness—and not the most important part.

Church Shoes and the Dining Room

Growing up, I (Geoff) had two pairs of sneakers: a nice pair and a not-so-nice pair. I wore the nice pair of sneakers to church on Sundays and to other fancy events. They were set apart for special occasions. The other pair I wore to school, the park, and the mall—they were for everyday use. Once the nice pair started getting too dirty to clean up and lost their luster, they were demoted to everyday status, and I would go out and buy a new pair. The new pair became the nice pair, and the cycle would repeat.

When I (Cyd) was growing up there was a room in our house set apart for entertaining special guests. The carpet was perfectly white. The furniture didn't have a single stain. Our family wasn't allowed to hang out in there or to get anything dirty. The door was always closed as a reminder that this place was special. We jokingly called it "the holy of holies" because it felt like violating that space carried the penalty of death.

Many of us have these kinds of things. Maybe instead of shoes or rooms, it's a favorite pen or special dishes—something reserved for special purposes or special occasions.

In biblical terms this is the difference between what is holy and what is common. Some things are set apart for a special purpose. Or to say it differently, they are *devoted* to a special purpose. When something is devoted to God's purposes, it's called holy.

Devoted to a Purpose

When God calls Israel to be holy, he is calling them to be devoted to a special purpose. We already explored this purpose in chapter four, when we talked about God making Adam and Eve his images, to rule and reign with him and to help all life flourish.

After Adam and Eve failed in this calling, God says to Israel, "Although the whole earth is mine, you will be for me a kingdom of priests and a holy nation" (Exodus 19:5-6 NIV). God is the King. And now Israel is the image of God in the world. Being a "kingdom of priests" is all about tending the fireplace of God's presence, the tabernacle (see chap. 7).

But Israel is also called to be a "holy nation." What does that mean?

Making God's Name Known

Israel was called to a special task. They were supposed to be devoted to God so that God's name would be proclaimed in all the earth (Exodus 9:16).

Remember that Adam and Eve were idols of God—living statues showing where God's rule and reign extended. Another way of saying this is that Adam and Eve were supposed to make God's name known in all the earth. That job now passed to Israel. Their imaging of God, extending his rule and reign and bringing his blessing, was for the sake of making his name known to all nations.

Is this different from any other ancient ruler? Don't all tyrannical kings want to be famous? Doesn't every dictator want his name known to the ends of the earth? Isn't this a pretty self-centered agenda?

For humans, yes. But not for God. God's name is different from any other. When God reveals himself to Moses, God calls himself "the compassionate and gracious God, slow to anger, abounding in love and faithfulness" (Exodus 34:4-6 NIV).

This compassionate and gracious God spoke life into all creatures. This is the God who longs to see all living things flourish and thrive. This is the God who gave Adam and Eve the opportunity to join him in that work of flourishing life. When they fell into death, this compassionate and gracious God set a plan in motion to offer his presence again to all people, and to restore their purpose in the world. This is the God who sought out Abraham, waiting and wandering, and told Abraham that he and his descendants would be a blessing to all nations.

To live under God's name is to truly live. To live under God's name is to bless others, not oppress them. To live under God's name is to be liberated, not enslaved. It is to be loved, not discarded. In other words, God is unlike any other leader or any other god.

Devoted to Bless

So when God says that Israel will be a blessing to all nations, it means his flourishing life will flow through his people (his images) to all nations. When this happens, God's ways will be "known on the earth" and God's "saving power among all the nations." Indeed, all the nations will be "glad and sing for joy" because of God (Psalm 67:4).

The prophet Isaiah gives us the most striking word about God's blessing through Israel. As you read this, remember that Egypt and Assyria were bitter rivals who took turns enslaving Israel.

> On that day there will be a highway from Egypt to Assyria, and the Assyrian will come into Egypt, and the Egyptian into Assyria, and the Egyptians will worship with the Assyrians.
>
> On that day Israel will be the third with Egypt and Assyria, a blessing in the midst of the earth, whom the LORD of hosts has blessed, saying, "Blessed be Egypt my people, and Assyria the work of my hands, and Israel my heritage." (Isaiah 19:23-25)

A blessing in the midst of the earth! Israel is tasked with bringing peace to warring nations. As the ones who know the goodness of God, Israel will proclaim the good name of God to the world. This is their job. This is their purpose: To join God in bringing blessing to all nations. To be peacemakers, and to bring life and peace where there is only violence and death.

This is Israel's holiness. They are set apart, but not to run and hide or to remove themselves from the world, desperate to stay clean and untainted by the nations. No. They were called to be devoted to

God—set apart for a special purpose. Israel was devoted to God for the sake of the world.

What does devotion look like?

Which Way Are You Headed?

Being devoted to God is like being oriented in a particular direction.

I (Geoff) was listening to the *Hidden Brain* podcast one day while driving home from teaching. I heard a fascinating story about an aboriginal people in Australia whose language is built around their sense of direction.

In the language of this tribe there isn't a word for "hello." Instead, when you greet someone, you say, "Which way are you heading?" The person answers by stating the exact direction they are facing: north, south, east, or west. "To get past hello, you have to know which way you're heading."[1]

Because everyday greetings are based on a person's sense of direction, children as young as four are proficient at knowing the difference between north by northwest and true north—something that most adults in the United States can't do (myself included).

Because they have grown up constantly orienting themselves within the larger landscape, they are always aware that they are part of something much bigger than themselves. In their daily interactions members of this tribe know where they are, *and* they know where they are heading.

Oriented to Holiness

We need to think of God's call to holiness in the same way—as an orientation, a direction we are heading.

Israel was not merely called to be separate from the other nations; they were to be devoted to God—oriented exclusively toward God and God's way of life. This way of life was given in the Law.

God gave his Law to Israel so they would know right from wrong, good from evil. Just like children growing up in that Australian tribe can orient themselves toward true north, God's law oriented Israel toward God's way of life and freedom. Because God is the author of life, Israel was to be oriented toward life. Because God is the giver of freedom, Israel was to be oriented toward freedom. In other words, just as God is holy, Israel too must be holy. And they would do this so the nations would know the life-giving ways of God.

When all the peoples and nations of the world are going this way and that way, Israel was meant to stay directed toward God. Israel is to be holy as God is holy by being distinct and different—by being directed toward and devoted to God. They not only needed to know where they are (with God) but also where they are heading (toward life), so that all nations might follow along.

In this way Israel would make God's name known to all the nations. They would become a blessing to all nations, leading them to God's way of life. In this way God's blessings would again bless all people. This would be the fulfillment of God's promise to Abraham—that God would bless Abraham in order to make him a blessing to all people.

The Family Business

God gave his presence to Israel so they could become partners in his purposes. He offered Israel a loving connection so they could contribute to the blessing of the world. This is how God's presence and purpose are supposed to work together. God's presence and purpose don't come with a heavy-handed demand for perfection. They come with an invitation into God's family and a share in the family business.

This isn't merely Israel's purpose. It's their joy. This participation in the blessing of all nations is also the return to the joy that God intends for them. In the Psalms we see that when all the nations learn about God through the life of Israel, all the earth will sing for joy (Psalm 66).

Joy is knowing that you're with someone who is glad to be with you. Israel, whom God was glad to be with, was intended to bring that gladness to all nations that they might also experience the joy of knowing the One who is always glad to be with them. Israel—by dwelling in the presence of God—is regaining a secure foundation for joy. And this joy leads them outward to courageously witness to the ways of God.

Not a Bad Boss

Some of us worry that God is a demanding taskmaster, always ready to point out our mistakes. With this image in mind it's easy to believe God must not like us very much, even if he might love us in a distant kind of way. How could he like us? We keep messing things up.

If God, the King, is a taskmaster, then the call to holiness feels more like a curse than kindness, more like a burden than a blessing. So many of us labor under the illusion that we must make God happy by being perfect. And not just God but others in our lives too. We struggle to fulfill countless routines and expectations in the hope they will make us acceptable, lovable. If only we lose weight or make more money or get married, then our parents or spouse or coworkers will like us better. They won't be ashamed of us.

But God isn't a demanding taskmaster, like Cyd's clarinet teacher at camp. God's purposes for us are to pursue life and point others toward that life. God's call to holiness is a call to be oriented toward—devoted to—life with him. The call to holiness isn't a rejection of the world. It is the call to be devoted to God for the sake of the world.

Practice: Examen

Go back to your joy place that you remembered in part one. Remember all the details again. Keep remembering until you experience the peace and delight of that place. Ask God to meet you there. Thank him for coming to you. Ask him to show you how you've been oriented toward life and devoted toward blessing the world in the last few days. Celebrate those moments. Now ask him to show you how you've been oriented toward death, devoted to the destruction of yourself, others, the world around you. Lament those with him. Confess your sin and receive his forgiveness. Let him remind you that you still belong with him and he still wants you to be part of the family business.

Reflection

How have you thought of God's holiness throughout your life as a believer?

How have you experienced the command to be holy?

How has reading this chapter and thinking of holiness as devotion or orientation shifted your thinking about what it means to be holy?

Song

As you listen to "Heaven on Earth" by Stars Go Dim, consider how you are being set apart for the family business of bringing heaven to earth.

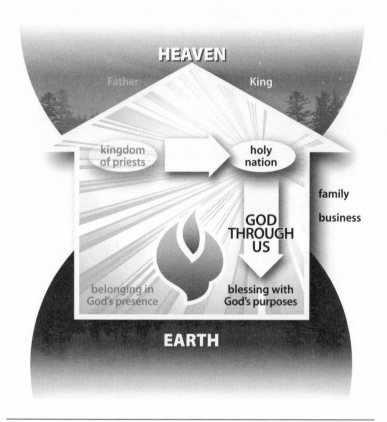

Through Israel, God's holy nation, God blesses the world with his purposes.

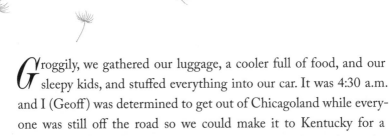

Chapter Nine

Is God Done with Me?

*G*roggily, we gathered our luggage, a cooler full of food, and our sleepy kids, and stuffed everything into our car. It was 4:30 a.m. and I (Geoff) was determined to get out of Chicagoland while everyone was still off the road so we could make it to Kentucky for a conference. About forty-five minutes later we were flying down the highway out of Chicagoland when Cyd shouted, "Aren't you getting off?"

About half an hour earlier, while I was still waking up, there had been a highway interchange where the exit lanes ran parallel to the through lines for about a half mile. In my early morning haze I had nearly missed the interchange. But because the exit lanes run parallel for so long, I had gently crossed through the "no man's land" part of the ramp and made the exit. Sure, it was less than legal, but it kept us from missing the exit, and it wasn't dangerous at all. Crisis averted.

Because of my experience on that exit, when Cyd asked, "Aren't you getting off?" I thought this new exit would be no problem. I turned the car sharply toward the exit ramp.

But this time the ramp was extremely short. Instead of an expanse of asphalt, I was suddenly faced with a half dozen orange barrels protecting a concrete barrier. So I yanked the wheel even farther to the right to avoid them. But while the other ramp had stayed on the same level, this exit ramp dropped abruptly downhill, and the car began pulling farther to the right, threatening to go down the embankment. So to keep the car from running off the far right side of the exit ramp, I yanked the wheel back left.

That's when we started spinning out of control.

When we stopped we were facing oncoming traffic and the highway we had just exited. Miraculously, the only damage to the car was a scraped door as the car had come to rest on a guardrail.

Almost missing the first exit had been no big deal. So when I almost missed the second exit, I assumed I could break the law again. But that assumption nearly rolled the car—and nearly killed my family.

The lane markers and exit lines aren't on the road because a sadistic rule maker demands that we follow rules. They're there to keep us alive. I made an exception to the rules the first time and didn't die. So why not a second time?

The Patterns We Make

We've all experienced times when we've done something that was either slightly illegal, slightly antisocial, or slightly self-destructive. Maybe we told a little lie, took a dollar from our brother's dresser, had a beer before we were of legal age, went a little further with our boyfriend than we intended to, didn't follow proper procedure at work, took credit for someone else's contribution, took someone else's prescription medication, or drove twenty miles per hour over the speed limit. Whatever it was, we got away with it. Nothing bad happened. There was no consequence. And so we did it again. And again . . . and again.

This is the way sinful patterns take hold in our lives. When I (Cyd) was fifteen, a friend offered me a cigarette. I had been told that smoking would kill me. But my friend had started smoking and she wasn't dead yet, so I tried it. And I didn't die. I didn't get arrested. My parents didn't find out. So I did it again. And again, and again. Eventually, I was buying my own packs. I was getting away with it, and nothing bad was happening.

I told myself I didn't *need* to smoke, I only *liked* to smoke. I didn't smoke every day, so it wasn't an addiction. But when I went to college I began smoking every day. Every morning. Between classes. After meals. On study breaks. A concerned friend urged me to consider quitting. But I insisted I wasn't addicted. So she challenged me to go without smoking for a week to prove it. I couldn't do it. I made it for about twelve hours before I couldn't concentrate on the paper I needed to write.

What began as a one-time thing became an occasional thing, then a habit, and finally an addiction. It took me years to finally break the hold that cigarettes had on me.

Anyone who has ever struggled with any kind of addiction (chemical, physical, emotional) knows this. You never start something intending to become addicted. Before we know it, we're stuck—bound and enslaved by something we never thought of as powerful. This is the reign of death at work in us and through us.

Once we fall into the grip of sin, we want to hide it. We want to deny it. Usually, we feel awful about it. How could we be so stupid? How could we mess up like this again? We begin to condemn ourselves. And we distance ourselves from the people who love us and could help us—especially God. We're so ashamed of ourselves that, like Adam and Eve, we hide—believing God will condemn us. This is the world of shame, making us feel deficient and defective.

What does God think of us when little by little we turn from him and choose sin instead? What does God feel about us when we step onto the way of death by abandoning his presence and purposes?

Israel Walks the Way of Death

Israel—just like all of us—chose the way of death. Even though God had placed them in his presence and given them a divine purpose, they started walking in the opposite direction, away from life. And it all started with baby steps.

Israel started slipping little by little. The priests didn't follow the instructions for maintaining God's presence as carefully as they had at first. The people started mixing with the nations more than they should have. Israel built little altars to little idols. People started acting unjustly, and leaders started abusing their power. They stopped caring for the wanderers and the unwanted in their midst.

Instead of bearing witness to God's love, justice, and mercy, Israel was becoming greedy, corrupt, and oppressive.

And nothing drastic happened. Israel wasn't destroyed. They didn't die. There were no apparent consequences. They were getting away with it. So Israel kept going further and further down the path of death.

Israel was called to be the image of God in the world, to dwell in God's presence and fulfill his purposes. But Israel was slowly abandoning God. Israel exchanged God's glorious presence for the presence of false idols. Time after time God called Israel back to faithfulness. And time after time Israel turned from God's way of life and freedom, returning to the land of slavery and death.

Eventually, Israel entered the darkest period of its history—the exile.

The exile is when God allowed other nations to destroy Israel and march its best and brightest off to slavery—first to Assyria in the north and then to Babylon in the east.

In a sense, the exile is when Israel died.

If God Did It to Israel . . .

We have a good friend who often points to the exile as proof that God is always on the edge of being done with her. She believes that deep down God doesn't like her but is just putting up with her. She believes that God puts up with her stupidity for now, but someday God's going to tire of her and kick her out of the kingdom. If he did it to Israel, she says, why wouldn't he do it to me?

Maybe you can relate to our friend.

If you're prone to think of God as a strict disciplinarian, then the exile seems to prove it. If God's relationship with Israel is all about keeping rules and regulations, keeping as holy as possible in a sinful world, then it's easy to think of God's harsh measures as an essential part of who God is. It's easy to think that God is actually like this all of the time, ready to snap at the smallest infraction, ready to blow up when you keep screwing up.

Maybe you think all this emphasis on living in God's presence and fulfilling his purposes isn't really the most important part of the story. Maybe you think we've been deluding ourselves and focusing on the wrong thing. As you've been reading this book, maybe you've had a constant thought that sounds something like, *Yes, but . . .* Yes, but isn't God holy and just? Yes, but doesn't God's wrath burn against sin? Yes, but doesn't the exile show that God is jealous to protect his glory?

Not Punishment but Resurrection

But before we assume that God doesn't like us because of the exile, we need to remember that the exile isn't primarily about God punishing sin but about God resurrecting the dead. To understand this, we need to unpack things a little.

The prophet Ezekiel helps us understand why God allowed Israel to be taken into exile.

Israel was called to dwell in God's presence and to live according to his purposes. But they abandoned God's presence and abdicated his purposes. Let's unpack these two things.

Abandoning God's presence. The first reason for the exile was that Israel broke God's heart by abandoning his presence. We need to keep the relationship between God and Israel front and center. If we don't, then our understanding of the exile—and the entire Old Testament—will be distorted. The prophet Ezekiel does this in a striking allegory about Israel and God being married to each other in Ezekiel 16.

Ezekiel personifies Israel as an abandoned baby girl dying on the roadside, rejected and neglected. God passes by and, moved by love, nurtures the dying baby back to health. When she grows up, God comes to marry her. God washes and dresses her in fine clothes of rich fabric and adorns her with bracelets and rings and a crown of fine jewels. He gives her fine food to eat and drink. In love, God makes a beautiful queen out of an abandoned child. And not just a royal queen—a priestly queen.

We need to remember that the prophet Ezekiel was also a priest trained in the temple. So when Ezekiel describes how God adorns and feeds Israel, he uses words that describe the clothing and food of the high priest.[1] Ezekiel reminds us that Israel was God's precious bride who was supposed to dwell in God's presence forever—just like Adam and Eve were meant to do. Ezekiel is reminding Israel that they are a royal priesthood and a holy nation in relationship with the God who loves them.

But the honeymoon didn't last long. According to Ezekiel, Israel took all the good gifts God had given—the fine clothing, expensive jewelry, and choice food—and started offering these to false idols. Israel broke her marriage to God by worshiping other gods. As Ezekiel and many other prophets would say, Israel committed adultery against God by following after these other gods. Israel broke God's heart by being unfaithful—by committing adultery through idolatry.

Because God is the God of love, it is against his character to force Israel to stay with him. Because Israel was set on pursuing other gods, God stepped aside and allowed Israel to have her way. But in abandoning God's presence, Israel was also abandoning God's protection. God allowed the other nations, who were always bent on domination and abuse, to have their way with Israel. And this meant Israel was conquered and carried off into exile.

This is the first reason for the exile. God allowed Israel to have what she chose—to be free from his presence. Israel didn't realize that by choosing to separate herself from God, she was choosing self-destruction and death. Like Adam and Eve, Israel abandoned the God of life and entered the realm of death.

Abdicating God's purposes. The second reason for the exile had to do with Israel's purpose in the world. Israel was supposed to reveal

God's character to the nations and thereby draw the other nations in to the God of life. But through her wickedness, Israel abdicated her purpose. By her actions, Israel was lying to the nations about who God was. As Ezekiel says quite often, Israel was profaning God's name among the nations (Ezekiel 20:9-24; 22:6-26; 36:20-23).

What does it mean that Israel was profaning God's name?

Bobo Dolls

To help us understand this, let's look at a 1961 psychology study by Albert Bandura at Stanford University. Bandura was curious about how witnessing aggression could affect preschool children.

Children were given opportunities to play with several different toys after witnessing an adult interacting with a Bobo doll. A Bobo doll is one of those inflatable toys with a heavy base so that when it is pushed over it stands back up by itself. Sometimes the adult would just ignore the Bobo doll. But other times the adult would pick up a hammer and physically and verbally assault the Bobo doll. And then sometimes the adult was punished for mistreating the doll. But other times the adult wasn't punished.

Interestingly—or perhaps predictably—the children who had seen the adult ignore the doll also ignored it when they had playtime. But the children who had seen the adult get away with verbally and physically assaulting the doll repeated the same behavior as soon as they got in the playroom. And the children didn't do this reluctantly. They did it exuberantly.[2]

We learn how to treat people by watching how other people interact with each other. When we see bad behavior punished, we avoid punishment by avoiding the behavior. But when we see people get away with bad behavior, we will expect to be immune to consequences also—like when I (Cyd) saw my friend smoking without getting caught.

The Adult in the Room

God called Israel to be the adult in a room filled with children. Israel was supposed to avoid (or ignore) the ways of sin and death so other nations would know the ways of God for humanity. Israel was supposed to live according to God's love, mercy, and justice. Israel was supposed to be the example of good behavior, of loving God and others, of living in God's presence and pursuing God's purposes.

But instead Israel picked up the hammer and punched the doll in the face. Instead of defending the poor and the powerless, Israel's leaders abused their power. Instead of showing the world the joy of living in God's presence, they abandoned God for idols. Instead of caring for the wandering and the unwanted, Israel took advantage of those they were called to bless. Instead of living out God's purpose for them, Israel abdicated their mission. They were telling lies about God.

By following other gods, Israel was saying that God doesn't care how we live. By abusing the poor and the neglected, Israel was saying that God doesn't care about the weak and downtrodden. By living on the way of death, Israel was saying that God doesn't care about life.

This is what Ezekiel means when he says that Israel is profaning God's name. They were telling lies about who God is and what God cares about.

Some Maintenance Required

So what is God going to do? How is he going to show Israel and everyone else that this is not the way to live? How is God going to clean up his name once it's been dragged through the mud of sin and death?

Israel had chosen the way that leads to death. So God let Israel die. But he did this to show that he isn't a God who sides with death.

That probably sounds harsh. It might reinforce the idea that God is a harsh disciplinarian who delights in finding fault and punishing sin. It probably sounds like God's justice and holiness are greater than God's love.

Sometimes we worry that if we sin one too many times, God will just hang us out to dry—God will let us just die, just like he did to Israel.

Before we think this confirms our worst fears about God, we need to consider the alternatives.

As we saw in chapter seven, God's presence is like a fire God placed within a specially built fireplace. That was called the tabernacle and later the temple. This fireplace for God's glory was a place of blessing for Israel, and this blessing was supposed to overflow to all nations. The tabernacle/temple made it safe enough for the fiery presence of God to dwell among sinful humanity.

Like all fireplaces, this one needed to be properly maintained. The tabernacle (and later the temple) was maintained by the priests who taught the Law and offered the sacrifices. But the work of maintaining the place of God's presence was not only a job for the priests. All of Israel was supposed to help in maintaining the place of God's presence by living holy lives—by living according to the way of life outlined in the Law. This was especially true of Israel's leaders, who had the power to influence whether the people would follow God's way of life or the way of death.

What happens when a fireplace is not properly maintained? It becomes dangerous. It becomes hazardous. Smoke starts flowing back into the house. Hot embers shoot up and land on the roof. A broken fireplace can burn down the entire house.

God could have kept the fire burning in Israel. But with Israel's sin corrupting the place of God's presence, the fireplace was broken, and the fire was going to break out and burn down the entire house— and not just the house of Israel but all of creation.

God didn't want to burn down the house of creation. God is the God of life. He wants life to reign. He longs for the re-creation of all things. He wants to dwell with humanity again and to bless humanity again.

Instead of letting the fire burn and threaten the entire house, the only other option was to let the fire go out. He could remove his presence from the temple and withdraw his glory from Israel. This way the damaged fireplace wouldn't burn down the house of creation. Rather than letting all people suffer the way of death, God removed his glory from Israel for a time (Ezekiel 10:1–11:25).

Remember that God had to remove Adam and Eve from his presence in the Garden because they no longer had the capacity to bear his presence, to hold his breath of life? In the same way God had to remove his presence from the crumbling fireplace of the temple. His glory left Israel. He hid his face (Ezekiel 39:21-24).

The fire that brought Israel life was put out. And now Israel experienced the consequences of their abuse and abandonment—just as Adam and Eve had. And as in Eden, what looks like God being fed up is actually God choosing to allow his people to be free—respecting their choices, even when it leads to death.

But how does all of this rehabilitate God's name, the name that Israel profaned? How would God still be known as loving and merciful, as the one who cares for the weak, wandering, and unwanted, if he lets his own people die?

The One Who Raises the Dead

How is a good and merciful God revealed in the death of Israel? How is God revealed as the one who longs to be *with us* if he lets Israel die?

Too often we focus on the first thing God does and we miss the second thing. We focus on what God allows to happen and we miss what God is longing to happen. The second thing is what God really wants to do; the second thing reveals God's heart of love.

The truth is that God doesn't merely long to be known as holy and just, as the one who takes sin seriously. Those things are true. That's the first thing. And we shouldn't forget it.

But more importantly, God desires to be known as the one who raises the dead.

Our God is the God of the resurrection, the God of second chances, of bringing people back from the brink. He is the God who longs to be with us even in the darkest places of rebellion and death. God doesn't kill sinners; he raises them from the dead! God isn't revolted by sinners; he gathers them in. He doesn't rejoice in punishment; he delights in mercy.

The exile, the death of Israel, doesn't primarily reveal God's justice (although it does do that). It shows us a God who raises the dead, who doesn't quit, who won't give up.

Dry Bones

Resurrection is what Ezekiel's famous "Valley of Dry Bones" vision is all about. God is showing Ezekiel that even though Israel has died, God is going to raise them from the dead.

In Ezekiel 37, Ezekiel reveals how God took him in a vision to a valley filled with bones scattered about. God asks Ezekiel if the dry bones could live again. And Ezekiel, even after seeing two visions of God's glory and a bunch of crazy angels, is unsure. He throws the question back to God, saying, "Lord, only you know."

God doesn't immediately jump in and bring the dead bones to life. Instead, he partners with Ezekiel. He tells Ezekiel to prophesy—to speak words of life over the dead bones. And when Ezekiel speaks, the scattered bones gather together, they connect into bodies, and they are covered by flesh. Then Ezekiel speaks again and the breath of life flows into the dead bodies, and they all stand up alive and well.

And then God gives Ezekiel the interpretation of the vision. Israel is crying out to God (as many of us do today), "Our bones are dried up, and our hope is lost." And God answers by saying, I am going to "open your graves, and bring you up from your graves. . . . I will put my Spirit within you, and you shall live" (Ezekiel 37:13-14). And when God brings Israel back to life, God's presence will be with them again. And when God's presence is with Israel again, then life and blessings will flow through Israel to all the nations again.

You see, God's final word to Israel is not death and destruction. It is resurrection and life.

Israel was called to dwell in God's presence. But they abandoned God for idols. Israel was called to bring God's blessing to all the nations, but Israel instead abdicated God's purpose. Israel headed straight toward death, and God allowed them to die. And yet God met them there, in the death they had freely chosen, and promised to raise them back to life.

Drastic Measures

Think of a doctor and a patient. The patient makes choices that lead to heart problems. The doctor encourages the patient to change his ways in order to improve his heart health. The patient says he will but doesn't. Finally, a small artery clogs. The patient experiences more fatigue than usual but ignores the signs. Finally, the patient has a full heart attack. The only way to save him is to cut his chest open, break his sternum, split his breastbone, spread his ribs, and cut the blockage out of the artery. This is done so the doctor can graft a new blood vessel in its place in order for the patient to live.

Imagine a person with no experience of modern medicine watching an open-heart surgery. It would probably look like a brutal form of execution. They might wonder what kind of society would allow such cruelty. But we know the doctor's intentions are not death but life.

When we look at the exile, we can see that Israel is like the patient who chose not to improve his health. But God wasn't willing to let Israel completely die. Instead, he performed open-heart surgery. Instead of seeing cruelty and violent torture, can we see the life-saving surgery that God begins in the exile?

Can you believe in the God who *allows* death but *desires* resurrection?

Practice: Palms Up, Palms Down

Go to your joy place. Invite God to join you. Sit comfortably with your palms up, resting on your knees. Offer yourself and everything you have to God in gratitude by offering your open hands to him. When something comes up that you feel overly attached to, turn your palms down as a way of symbolizing a refusal to worship that thing or allow it to become an idol in your life. Turn your palms back up and ask for God's grace and mercy to allow you to hold it lightly, with open hands instead of clenched fists. Continue to sit with God in this way, choosing to lay down idols and open your hands to offer all that God has given to you back to him.

Reflection

As you reflect on your own life, are there places where God has allowed you to experience devastation as a way of respecting your own wishes?

Think of those places and look for ways that God was also seeking to save your life. Notice the places where God has raised dry bones to life, brought beauty from ashes, and turned mourning into dancing in your story.

Song

As you listen to "Haven't Seen It Yet" by Danny Gokey, reflect on those places in your journey where you're waiting to see new life.

Like Adam and Eve, Israel chooses the way of death and God's house is destroyed again.

Part Three

God's Body

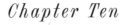

Chapter Ten

Is God Disgusted
with Me?

*W*e are about to make a big shift in the story of God and humanity. Up to this point we have seen heaven and earth overlapping in a particular place—Israel's temple. Now, we shift to heaven and earth overlapping in a person: Jesus, the Son of God.

But let's do a quick review.

Adam and Eve were created to live with God in the Garden. They were given everything they needed to enjoy God's presence and join his purposes. Adam and Eve were the children of the Father and welcomed in his home. And they were entrusted with the family business, the work of the kingdom of God.

And yet Adam and Eve turned from God, giving in to shame and sin—the shame that made them feel unworthy of God's presence and the sin that made them incapable of living in God's purpose. The blessing of life was lost when they chose death and darkness.

But God raised up Israel so that life and blessing would flow to all the nations. While all the nations were lost in the darkness of sin and death, God made Israel a royal priesthood and holy nation. Like Adam and Eve, God gave Israel his presence in the tabernacle and the temple, a new home where God would live with them. And God gave Israel the Law so the world would know God's purposes in order to flourish. Through Israel, God was again *God with us* and *God through us*.

And yet, like Adam and Eve, Israel left the path of life. They abandoned their work as priests of God's presence and abdicated their role as kings and queens of God's kingdom. They didn't act like well-loved children of a good Father. They didn't value being entrusted with an essential part of the family business. They exchanged all the goodness of God's family to follow worthless idols. They too chose to leave home. They too entered death.

Two times God has blessed humanity with his presence and purpose, and two times humanity has failed. And just like Adam and Eve and Israel, we too keep falling into sin and shame, abandoning God's presence and purpose.

What is God going to do?

The Paleo-South-Whole-Keto Diet

Whole 30, Vegan, Keto, Paleo. Chances are you've heard some of these names and they may trigger some kind of response in you. Maybe the response is "Yes!" Maybe it's "Give me a break!" Either way, we can all agree that our culture is obsessed with diets.

I (Cyd) have wrestled with eating for my entire life. Growing up, I watched my mom alternate between bowls of ice cream and plates of steamed broccoli. Throughout my life I have understood why she did this. Inheriting her genetic ability to pack on pounds in seconds flat, I have always needed to be aware of how much I eat and how much I exercise. Meanwhile, I live with a man and two teen-aged sons who can eat whatever they want, whenever they want, and still not carry a single ounce of extra body fat. The struggle is real.

And so I do my best to eat what *my* body wants and thrives on—which means avoiding lots of carbohydrates or dairy. But eventually I'll give in to that side of myself that just loves crusty white bread slathered with butter, a good craft cheese, and cheesecake drizzled with fresh berries (not all at the same time). And then the inevitable happens—my body rebels. I feel sluggish, bloated, achy, miserable. And I berate myself again for going against what I know is right for my body and caving in to the longing to enjoy the tastes I miss so much.

And so I swing back and forth on a pendulum. I live at peace in my body when I eat and exercise in ways that let me thrive. And then I resent my body and treat it with contempt, eating things as an act of war against myself. In those moments I long to have a blank slate for a body—one that holds no memory of the taste of cheese, the crunch of crusty bread, or the decadence of ice cream. If I could just start from scratch and eat only meat and vegetables, I would never know any other way.

Maybe you aren't wrestling with your body. Maybe you feel at war with your personality or with your dreams and ambitions or with your talents and calling. Chances are there's some part of you that you wish you could do away with or change. Why are we so often trying to change something about ourselves, something that is too much or not enough? Why do we wrestle so much with who we are, with our bodies, our personalities, hopes, and dreams?

Sin and Shame

The thing we are constantly wrestling with has a name: shame.

Remember that joy is the experience of being with someone who is always glad to be with us (chap. 1). Shame alerts us to a disconnection with someone we love—which is a good thing. When we become aware of the disconnection, we can seek out our loved one and repair the relationship. Shame can help us return to the joy where we are glad to be with each other. At its best, shame invites us to do the work to come back home and be in relationship with God and with others.

But shame is also extremely dangerous. It has the power to keep us from relationships with others. It has the power to keep us from finding a home. If we don't seek to repair our relationships, or if the other person refuses to repair the relationship, then we experience a permanent rupture. From this rupture comes the feeling of being unwanted, causing us to withdraw and hide even more.

The same thing can happen to our bodies. When we experience shame about our bodies, it's a sign that we're disconnected from them. We've begun to look at our bodies from the viewpoint of usefulness as if they were merely tools. When my body looks a certain way, it benefits me. When my body feels a certain way, it works for me. When my body no longer serves me the way I want it to, I become ashamed of my body. It's in my way. Some of us might think *If only my body were more fit, less flabby, stronger, smaller, bigger, and the like.*

Some of us can embrace our bodies, but we're ashamed of aspects of our personality we would rather not have. *If only I wasn't so intense, or so shy, or so analytical.*

Underneath all of this wishful thinking is a sentiment we probably don't want to speak out loud. *I don't want to be me.* And it reminds me of what I (Cyd) learned about strawberries when I lived in California.

Strawberry Fields

I love strawberries! As a kid growing up in Michigan, I loved going along to the farmer's market and buying little wooden quart boxes of strawberries fresh from the local farms. So when I moved to California's central coast and discovered that Watsonville is the nation's strawberry capital, I was thrilled. But when I learned about the process required to produce all of those strawberries, my delight in eating strawberries was lost.

The process includes two major parts: propagating the plants to preserve the perfect DNA and fumigating the soil to eliminate disease. All of the strawberries grown in the region are descendants of a tiny tissue sample snipped from a perfect plant and grown in a petri dish in a lab. That's why strawberries are so uniform in shape, size, color. All of the diversity and deformity have been bred out of the line. They are never allowed to reproduce naturally because there could be recessive traits or even mutations. Instead, they are carefully cloned for perfection.

Before the strawberries are put into the soil, the soil is injected with fumigants and then covered with plastic to keep the chemicals in the soil long enough to basically kill every living thing. This combination of sterile soil and replicated plants is what produces the bumper crops of strawberries month after month. Using this tried and true method, farmers can grow strawberries nearly year-round, getting identical results.

In summary: destroying all diversity *plus* killing the soil *equals* perfect strawberries.

Against Our Flesh

Without realizing it, we sometimes treat ourselves the same way and call it godliness. *If I could just get rid of this imperfection, if I could just hide these faults, if I could just ignore these mistakes, I would be more like Jesus. Then God would love me. If I wasn't so impulsive, clumsy, loud, quiet. If I was just a little thinner, a little richer, a little taller, had a little more hair, then I would be a good steward of my body.*

We want to destroy all the things that make us deformed and imperfect people and kill the bodies that carry the weirdness. If only we could eradicate the stuff that makes us feel unfit for the family of God and then start with a blank slate, then we would be able to get it right. Then we would belong in God's presence. Then we could accomplish God's purposes.

We can even think this is God's process for saving us from sin and shame. Just replace *me* with something perfect—get a perfect new plant, get some plastic to cover over the broken and shameful things, and get some chemicals to kill whatever is left.

In fact, sometimes it feels like salvation means putting off our skin. It feels like the Bible is telling us to get rid of our flesh—to get rid of our bodies. The apostle Paul seems to tell us this repeatedly. He says that in our baptism we put off the "body of the flesh" in order to be raised up in Christ (Colossians 2:11). Elsewhere Paul says that Jesus "condemned sin in the flesh" so we could walk in the Spirit (Romans 8:3). And to live according to the flesh means we are unable to please God because we are hostile toward him (Romans 8:6-8). And most simply,

"Those who belong to Christ Jesus have crucified the flesh with its passions and desires" (Galatians 5:24).

It seems clear. The flesh is bad!

God Doesn't Hate Our Flesh

If God wants to save us, it seems like he needs to destroy us or at least our flesh. God may love us, but it seems like he only likes part of us—the spiritual part.

This sounds like bad news.

But remember that all creation was originally made to be the dwelling place of God. God loves trees, plants, rivers, and bodies. God called it all good, according to his purpose in Genesis 1. But after the fall, we tend to orient ourselves toward shortcuts and easy solutions—like Eve's grasping for the fruit rather than seeking God's presence. This orientation toward fulfillment apart from God is what Paul means when he warns us not to set our minds on the flesh (Romans 8:5-6). He's urging us to turn away from quick solutions and cheap satisfaction (the things of the "flesh") and orient our hearts, minds, and physical bodies toward the life that is found only in God's presence.

The "flesh" that God's most concerned about is not skin and bone. It's our tendency toward self-centered desires and destructive actions. Our "body of the flesh" (Colossians 2:11) is our slavery and bondage to sin. But just as that bondage is not limited to our bodies, so our bodies are not inherently bad just because they are made of flesh.

Hiding Our Humanity

Killing off and hiding our humanity isn't God's plan. In fact, it fits more with our plans. Killing and hiding is humanity's plan for managing our shame, fear, and nakedness because of sin. Adam and Eve first started hiding when they were naked and ashamed. They wanted to cover themselves—they were hiding and denying who they were. And we've been doing the same thing ever since.

We hide the difficult things in our lives and assume God isn't really interested in redeeming them.

If we struggle with mental health issues, we hide it, telling ourselves that anything but the joy of the Lord is a sin. If we struggle with our body image because we don't fit the mold of the skinny supermodel or the six-pack superhero, then we try harder to hit the gym to slim down or bulk up. If we struggle with the ever-present shame of past abuse, we tell ourselves to ignore it and hide it because it should all be in the past anyway.

We seek perfection—like those perfect strawberries. We bleach the soil of our lives. We cover everything we don't like. And then we just assume that this is God's work of salvation.

But God doesn't hate our personalities and our bodies like we do. In fact, it was God's love for the world that compelled him to send his Son. Jesus took on our flesh so we could wear his flesh. He came in the flesh to save our flesh and all of creation with it.

God Became Flesh

John's Gospel uses the word *flesh* in a different sense than Paul does, and it is much more positive. The Gospel of John tells us that Jesus, the Word who is God, "became flesh and lived among us" (John 1:14). Both of these statements—that God became *flesh* and that God *lived among us*—are vitally important for us, our bodies, and our lives.

Lived among us. When John says the Word "lived among us" he is referring back to the tabernacle and temple of God, God's house. He is saying that in Jesus, God is *tabernacling* or *dwelling* among his people again.

This is the fulfillment of the prophecy made by Ezekiel. God gave Ezekiel the vision of the Valley of Dry Bones. In that vision Ezekiel saw that God is the God who raises the dead, not just the God who punishes sin. Immediately after this vision Ezekiel hears God make a promise to Israel: "I will establish [Israel] and increase their numbers, and I will put my sanctuary among them forever. My dwelling place

will be with them; I will be their God, and they will be my people"
(Ezekiel 37:26-27 NIV). In this amazing prophecy, God promises to
dwell with his people again—to be *God with us* again.

These promises are fulfilled in Jesus, God in a human body, heaven
and earth coming together in a person. In Jesus, God's presence has
come from heaven to earth. This is the promise of Immanuel, "God
with us" (Matthew 1:21-23 NIV). But this time, *God with us* is not in
a particular place (e.g., a garden or a temple) but is now walking, living,
breathing, speaking, touching. God with us is Jesus, the Word
made flesh.

Became flesh. We need to remember that Jesus didn't take on the
flesh of a supermodel or a superhero. He didn't take on the flesh of a
fancy king, a famous rock star, or a flashy corporate executive. God
took on the ordinary life of a normal person at a particular moment
in time. He was raised in a real family. As an adult he worked a real
job for over fifteen years—yes, at least fifteen years of hands-on, blue-
collar work before he began his public ministry.

So Jesus experienced the humdrum of human existence. He knows
and understands daily drudgery. He knows and understands the idi-
ocies and injustices of everyday life. He was normal in every way.

Here's the rundown of his (less than) average life.

- Jesus was born a Jew. That means he grew up as a marginalized
  person (at best) or an actively oppressed person (at worst) in the
  Roman Empire. His country was occupied by a hostile, foreign
  power. He was raised in a war zone. He knows what it is like to
  grow up in a dangerous situation.
- Jesus also grew up on the wrong side of the tracks, as it were. He
  was raised in the north, in Galilee. The cultural elites lived in the
  south, in Jerusalem. People teased him and his disciples
  for having funny accents. Jesus understands what it's like to be
  picked on for where he was from.
- Jesus also grew up under suspicion that he was an illegitimate
  child, a bastard son. People knew who his mom was, but they

weren't sure who the dad was. Everyone knew Jesus was being raised by a guy who wasn't his real father. Jesus understands living in a complicated family environment.

Let's add all this up for a moment.

Jesus—God living among us in the flesh—was raised in an occupied country, grew up on the wrong side of the tracks, and was mocked for being an illegitimate son. And all of this happened before he started his ministry. This is the flesh he took on to be with humanity, for our salvation. *God with us.*

In his earthly life Jesus experienced every aspect of our humanity. He knew the joy of friendship and the sorrow of betrayal. He had beloved family members to live with and relatives who died too soon. He was surrounded by crowds and yet abandoned by all. He was lavished with gold, frankincense, and myrrh and yet lived poor as dirt. He was understood and known by people he loved yet was misunderstood and called crazy by the same. He knew the joy of God's presence and the shame of God's absence. He lived a full life and yet died in agony. He experienced the full height and depth of human flesh.

God Attuned

Sometimes we are so eager to affirm the divinity of Jesus or to rush on to his death and resurrection that we don't soak in the significance of Jesus' humanity. Jesus knows and understands you—in your body, in flesh. God is attuned to us in the most intimate way possible.

Jesus understands what it is like to be human. As much as you say, "I don't want to be me," Jesus says, "I love you so much that I became like you!" Jesus came in the flesh to make us human again.

In chapter three we talked about mirror neurons. These neurons connect with what someone else is doing and help us to empathize and attune with what they are experiencing. Jesus—God in the flesh—has fully attuned to us so that we could become fully attuned to him. Jesus has fully connected with our humanity so that we could fully connect to his divinity. In this deep, neurological connection God is beginning to repair our capacity for his presence. By renewing our neural pathways through his attunement to us, God is repairing our foundation for joy. And by repairing our foundation for joy, God is renewing our humanity. We are becoming what we were always meant to be—truly human through connection with the truly divine.

The Battle Is Not Against Flesh and Blood

Some of us have given our humanity away. Some of us had our humanity taken away. For most of us it is some of both. In the sin and shame of losing our humanity, sometimes we fight back and sometimes we fake it. We bow to the pressures around us or we boil over in resentment. No matter how we respond, the truth is we are in a battle. And many times sin has the upper hand.

But our battle is not against flesh and blood. As the apostle Paul says, our battle is against the spiritual powers and forces of evil of this world (Ephesians 6:12). Too often we battle against our own flesh and blood, against ourselves. But this is not the true battle. Our bodies are the battleground in the cosmic war between heaven and hell, between life and death. The powers and evil forces try to turn our humanity against us, making us feel unworthy, unlovable, unimportant, unseen, and unknown. The powers and authorities say that we aren't good enough or that we're too much.

And they say that God agrees with them, that God thinks we really are unworthy, unlovable, and unimportant. They urge us to grasp at quick solutions to this shame rather than seek what God has to say about us. Our enemy wants to destroy our humanity, and along with it our incredible connection to God as ones who bear his image.

But the truth is that God has come in the flesh to overcome those powers and forces of evil, to overcome sin and shame. Jesus walks into our broken and embattled world and says to us, "I have carried shame and rejection, I have been abused and neglected, I have been misunderstood and ignored, but I didn't lose my humanity. And I can show you how." Jesus is offering us our true humanity again.

Whatever it is that makes you feel unworthy and unlovable and makes you hide in shame, Jesus knows it, and he is with you in it. He can make you whole because he took on real humanity. He became human to renew our humanity. Jesus brought heaven down to earth, bringing heaven into our very bodies. Just as God's home is now in a human body, God invites us to be at home in our bodies.

God in the flesh is with us, not disgusted with us. So let's give up our disgust for ourselves.

Practice: Palms Up, Palms Down Remix

Think about your joy place. Remember not only the details of the place but also any conversations you have had with God in this place since you started reading this book. Thank God for the ways he has already met you here. Invite him to join you again. Talk to him about how you feel about being in your body. Tell him what it's like for you to have your personality. As you notice things that you don't like or don't enjoy about yourself, turn your palms down as a way of giving those over to God and choosing to lay down your disgust. Turn your palms up and ask him how he would like to give your humanity back to you, how he might like to redeem you and your perspective.

Reflection

What is it like to think of Jesus as the Garden or the temple?

Is it strange to think of Jesus as the body, the person, that brings heaven and earth together in the same ways that the Garden and the temple did?

In Jesus, God creates a way to be with his people again—for the third time. How does this affect your understanding of why Jesus came?

Song

As you listen to "God With Us" by All Sons & Daughters, reflect on God taking on flesh to dwell with us.

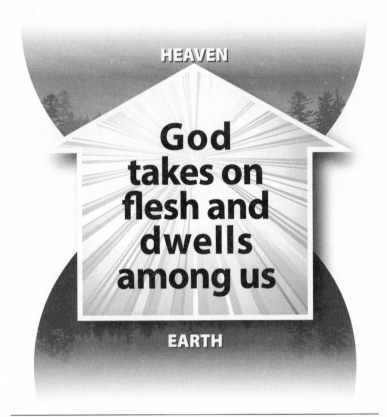

In Jesus (fully God and fully human), heaven and earth overlap once again, and God's joyous presence and purposes come to humanity once again.

Chapter Eleven

Am I Wanted?

*O*ur two boys, Soren and Tennyson, were born just seventeen months apart. Because they're so close in age, they grew up sharing the same friend groups—at church, in our home school community, in their theater company. Everywhere they went, they were together.

It was great when they were younger. It meant they always had a friend everywhere they went. If they felt shy or insecure, left out or excluded, each had his brother to boost his confidence and help him fit in. But as they got older, it got tougher. Soren didn't always want his younger brother around. And Tennyson felt overshadowed by his more outgoing older brother.

It didn't help that Soren was always big for his age, and Tennyson was generally smaller for his age. Even though they were less than a year and a half apart, people always thought Tennyson was three years younger than Soren. So people often treated Tennyson like a little kid even though he was into all the same things that Soren was.

Over time Tennyson developed the sense that nobody wanted to be friends with him. He figured they were just putting up with him because he was Soren's little brother. When they both walked into a room, everyone greeted Soren first and Tennyson second. He felt like an afterthought. He felt like he wasn't really wanted.

It was painful for him. No matter how much Soren tried to advocate for Tennyson and remind his friends that Tennyson wasn't that much younger, no matter how much Soren tried to celebrate his brother and encourage people to see him for his own person, Tennyson still felt overshadowed and unwanted.

Most of us can relate to that feeling. We do the hard work on a project and someone else gets the credit. We get passed over when someone less qualified gets the job. We don't get invited to a holiday party or faculty outing. We feel invisible next to someone who is better looking, more fit, more outgoing, more interesting. In different ways and in different places, we all have the experience of feeling unwanted—at home, at church, in the office, and even by God.

The Return of the Unwanted

But no matter how unwanted we feel, in Jesus we see God drawing near to us. Jesus draws near to the lowly and the forgotten, reminding them that they are welcome in the Father's family, a new family gathered from all people.

Everywhere Jesus goes he gathers in the unwanted people, those who are outcast and despised. We see Jesus reaching out and touching a leper (Mark 1:40-41), willing to embrace the untouchable and unclean. We see Jesus talking with an unwanted woman who had experienced several failed marriages and now lived with a man who wasn't her husband. Instead of despising her, Jesus offers her the living water that would satisfy her thirsty soul (John 4:1-42). We see Jesus heal Bartimaeus, a blind beggar crying out obnoxiously from the road (Mark 10:46-52). We see Jesus casting out the demons that drive a man to wander among tombs (Luke 8:26-39). And we even see Jesus talking with Zacchaeus, a tax collector who had probably overtaxed his entire village for years—if there was ever a man people didn't want around, it was Zacchaeus. Jesus even invites himself over to Zacchaeus's house, a high honor for such a detested man (Luke 19:1-10).

This should all sound familiar. In chapter six, when we talked about God returning his presence and purpose through Abraham and Sarah, we focused on how God worked through their waiting and their wandering. And we talked about how God revealed himself to Hagar when she felt so unwanted. This all sounds familiar because this is how God always works.

And God does it again through his Son. God returns his presence and purpose to humanity. After Israel's exile, God's glorious presence never returned to the temple in the same way as before. The people have been waiting for a long time for God to come back and reestablish his presence and purpose again in Israel and for all humanity. But in Jesus, God comes back as a person.

What difference does it actually make for us?

We find the answer in the baptism of Jesus.

The Baptism of Jesus

In the baptism of Jesus we see the heart of the Father delighting in his Son. Jesus can welcome the wandering and unwanted from this place of the Father's delight. He knows he belongs, and he extends that belonging to all the world.

The place of Jesus' baptism is significant. Jesus doesn't get baptized in the temple, in a synagogue, or in a big city. He is baptized in the Jordan River. The Jordan is the same river the people had to cross to get into the Promised Land after the exodus. The priests stepped into this river, carrying the ark of the covenant, the place of God's presence, and the waters roll back so they can walk through on dry land. The people then build an altar there so they can tell their children the story for generations to come. And when the people return from exile, they cross this same river to get back home. This river was a powerful place in Israel's history, a marker of new beginnings.

So when Jesus put his feet in the Jordan River, just imagine the angels were holding their breath, eager to see what new beginning would happen next. John baptizes Jesus. As Jesus is coming up out of the water, the moment arrives. The heavens are torn apart, the Holy Spirit descends on him, and the new beginning begins. We know this because of the words spoken from heaven over Jesus.

Words of Delight

It always begins with words. In the beginning God created the heavens and the earth by speaking—by the Word of God. And Jesus himself is the Word who has taken on flesh to dwell among us. Now, at Jesus' baptism, the Father speaks over the Son, just as God had spoken over creation. And the words he speaks are some of the most important words we hear in the Bible.

As the Holy Spirit comes to rest on Jesus, the Father's voice from heaven says, "You are my Son, the Beloved; with you I am well pleased" (Mark 1:11). This event is a defining moment for humanity.

Before Jesus has done anything significant, before anyone was healed or any demons were cast out, before he had preached any sermons or told any parables, before he had answered anyone's question with another question, before he had called out the Pharisees or cleared out the temple, or laid down his life on the cross and defeated death—before he had done any of these things, the Father delights in the Son: "With you I am well pleased."

Imagine the gladness and joy you would feel if the most important person in the world to you said they love you and are pleased with you. And imagine they say this to you just because you are sitting there, not because you had done something amazing, not because you're so easy to talk to, not because you dress sharply or know all about contemporary art, not because you finished the newest proposal or closed the latest deal, or did everything they asked you to do in just the way they expected—but just because they are pleased to be around you. This is the essence of joy.

The joy of the Father—revealed in his words and the witness of the Spirit resting on him—was the foundation of Jesus' life. The joy of the Father, who delighted in the presence of the Son, was the secure connection from which Jesus could welcome the unwanted, from which he could walk with the wandering, from which he could wash the wounded and encourage the broken hearted. This joy and gladness guided his ministry as the unshakable place he ministered from to the weak and the weary, to the fakers and the forgotten. No matter what kind of distress Jesus experienced, he could always return to joy in the delight of his Father.

And Jesus' mission was to bring others into the joyful family of the Father so they could hear the same words from the Father, "with you I am well pleased."

Where's the Party?

People loved being around Jesus.

Sometimes we get the idea that Jesus was somber and serious all the time. We probably get this from pastors and preachers who act that way. But wherever Jesus went, a party would break out. Even at his birth, the angel declared that they were bringing "good news of great joy for all the people" (Luke 2:10). Jesus got in trouble because the religious leaders thought he did too much feasting and not enough fasting, too much partying and not enough praying (Luke 7:34).

So why did people love being with Jesus?

We need to go back to our understanding of joy. Joy is the experience of being in the presence of someone who is glad to be with us. By this definition, Jesus is a joy bringer. As he encounters those who are unwanted, they experience the joy of acceptance. As he welcomes the wandering, they experience the joy of finding a family. And as Jesus brings healing to the waiting, they experience the joy of being seen and known. It's all about the joy of being connected with the God who says, "You are the Beloved. With you, I am well pleased."

Jesus lives from this place of joy, and he knows that the work of heaven is to gather more and more children into the joy of being part of the Father's family.

In Luke 15 Jesus tells three stories of lost things being found—a sheep, a coin, and a son. In each parable there is unspeakable joy when the lost thing is found. When the sheep is found, Jesus says that there will be "joy in heaven over one sinner who repents" (Luke 15:7). When the coin is found, Jesus says there is "joy in the presence of the angels of God over one sinner who repents" (Luke 15:10). And when the son returns home, there is a huge party where everyone celebrates and rejoices because the son "was dead and has come to life; he was lost and has been found" (Luke 15:32).

All who are seeking—something, anything—find joy in the presence of Jesus. The lost joy of creation, the lost joy of living in God's home, bursts forth through Jesus. He brings the presence of God to all the lost and broken places, and restores the joy that was intended from the beginning.

But some of us have stopped seeking. We've given up on the idea of even being wanted.

Learning to Live Without

When I (Cyd) was a little girl—fifteen months old—my father was killed in a car accident. My mother suddenly found herself a single mom with two little girls under the age of four. We lived in Michigan, but my mom's parents were in Washington state, and her best friend was in New Mexico. I can only imagine how alone she felt and how terrifying the world must have suddenly seemed. But she did what she needed to do. She put on a brave face. She continued to teach in a classroom and be a strong parent for my sister and me.

A few years after this tragedy, when I was four, she went to visit her best friend in the Philippines. She needed a place to grieve, to mourn, to just be. She needed a break from caring for others so she could care for herself. While she was gone, my sister and I needed someone to look after us. My grandparents were glad to step in. From the stories my grandparents told me about this season, I was miserable when my mom first left. I regularly asked about where she had gone and when she would come back.

But after a while I stopped asking where my mom was. I got used to life with my grandparents. My mom's absence bothered me less and less. I was finding a new normal.

When my mom finally returned, I didn't run to her. I didn't greet her with hugs and kisses. I didn't shout from the rooftops, "I'm so glad you're home!" Instead, I just kept playing with my toys as if a stranger had come to visit. When my grandma encouraged me to go "give your mom a hug," I clung to my grandma and refused to greet my mom. My little mind and heart were punishing her for leaving me. She had hurt me, and I had learned to live without her. At least, that's what I thought.

The same thing can happen with God.

Invited to Joy

We have been hurt and have felt so unwanted and unwelcome for so long that living without joy has become our new normal. We have become so used to our sin and shame that we no longer seek joyful connection. We no longer expect the presence of someone who delights in us. We've learned to expect less out of life. We've learned to fill the void with other things.

But these things are faulty substitutes. They lead to deeper bouts of anxiety and depression, of frantic striving and furious outbursts, of exhaustion and misunderstanding, of sinful self-medication and self-destruction.

These substitutes fail because we were made for joy. We were made to be in the presence of the One who delights in us. We know this because we were made in the image of God. Being made in God's image means belonging in God's presence—and in his presence we find joy because he is always glad to be with us.

For those of us who have stopped looking for joyful connection anymore, Jesus comes. He comes as the true, tangible image of God.

He comes to the unwanted and unwelcome to remind us that we have a place in God's presence, that we belong with God, that we too are images of God. Jesus invites us to hope again that we are loved by God—and even more, that we are liked by God. Jesus invites us to hear the words of the Father over us, "You are my Beloved. With you, I am well pleased."

When You Have a Place

On a smaller scale we saw this change in our son Tennyson after we moved to Grand Rapids. He came home from a friend's house and his face was bright and alive as he proclaimed, "I have my own friends! I have a place." In being with people who were glad to be with him, Tennyson tasted an earthly, human picture of being wanted and enjoyed. His yearning for friendship had been met.

Every time we make a connection like this, it's the echo of the song of joy always playing in the background. And those connections are not just between human friends but ultimately point us toward a connection we can have in Christ alone—God with us—who is always glad to be with us and to help us return to joy.

Jesus' earthly journey was one of joy, and he brings joy still wherever his presence is found. But all of this joy is merely an appetizer of the feast to come when we will all be invited to the wedding feast of the Lamb. We will all be in the presence of the One who is always glad to be with us for the rest of our days. Then joy will no longer play in quiet tones underneath the action; it will be the center of everything. Where the Spirit of the Lord is, there is joy!

This is the joy of *God with us.*

Practice: Receiving the Father's Pleasure

Read the account of Jesus' baptism in Luke 3:21-22. After you've read it, close your eyes and imagine standing with Jesus in the waters of the Jordan. Feel the water around your waist. Feel the sun on your face and your body. You look up and suddenly the sky tears open like a rip in a piece of fabric and you see a bright dove descending toward you. It rests on you and you feel life surge through your whole body. A gentle voice of pure power speaks, "You are my daughter, my son. With you, I am well pleased." As someone who has put your faith in Christ, these words are as true of you as they are of Jesus. Notice any resistance you have to receiving them and take that resistance to your joy place and talk to God about that.

Reflection

Have you learned to live without joy and connection? Think about your relationships and consider whether you seek connection or whether you seek safe distance or something in between. Would you like to experience joy and connection with God?

Song

As you listen to "You Say" by Lauren Daigle, reflect on whose voice is loudest in you.

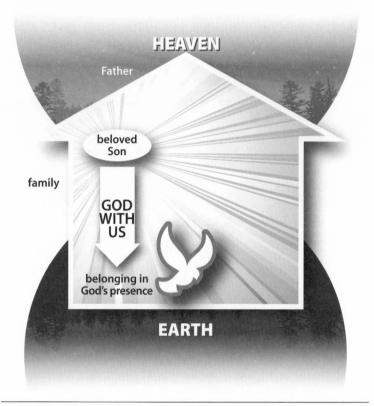

As the beloved Son of the Father, Jesus is bringing all of humanity back to the family of God—back into God's presence.

Chapter Twelve

Is This All There Is to Life?

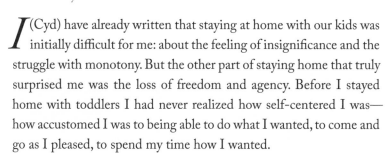

I (Cyd) have already written that staying at home with our kids was initially difficult for me: about the feeling of insignificance and the struggle with monotony. But the other part of staying home that truly surprised me was the loss of freedom and agency. Before I stayed home with toddlers I had never realized how self-centered I was—how accustomed I was to being able to do what I wanted, to come and go as I pleased, to spend my time how I wanted.

Because our kids are only seventeen months apart, my home life was formed and shaped by the rhythm of responding to two diaper-wearing, need-help-with-everything little people. When one cried, I tried to comfort. When one was hungry, I fed. When one was dirty, I cleaned. When one was rebelling, I disciplined. It was easy to make plans for the day but nearly impossible to keep them.

Up until this time I had been a fairly competent, organized human being with a clean house and an intentional calendar. Now, my circumstances forced me to give up control, to submit to the unpredictability of the day, and to go with the flow. I learned, for good or ill, to be a milk-producing, diaper-changing, entertainment-providing comforter.

My world felt small. It pinched and pressed in, reminding me daily that I was not my own person. I felt like these two needy toddlers owned me.

Maybe you've experienced something like this. Maybe a job was new and exciting and looked like the opportunity you had been waiting for, but now it's choking the life out of you, demanding overtime, and forcing you to work on tasks that aren't interesting to you. Maybe being a full-time student is a lot less fulfilling than you imagined, and now you'll be spending the rest of your life paying off those loans. Maybe you used to love serving others, but now you feel taken advantage of and unappreciated.

Whatever the case might be, at some point most of us experience the feeling that in some way our life does not truly belong to us. It feels like the best of our energy is spent following someone else's agenda or reaching after someone else's goals. Life is a letdown. *I have so much more potential than this!* we might think to ourselves.

Maybe you've thought about making a change, but you felt stuck. *What else can I do? This is just my life.* We keep doing what we're doing but have the sense there's something better out there, something more meaningful and significant than this.

Seeking Significance

Whether we know it or not, we are constantly trying to figure out whether we matter. We often answer it by looking at three things: what we do, what we have, and what people think of us.

If I get a lot done, then I am significant.

If I have lots of stuff, then I'm safe and secure.

If people really like me, then they'll keep me around.

But each of these ways of finding our identity leads us deeper into the anxiety that comes from our search for significance. Each of these ways of shaping who we are requires constant maintenance, constant upkeep. If who we are is based on what we do, what we have, or what people think of us, then we are constantly producing, possessing, and pleasing. Our worth and value are always in question when we fail to do the right thing, lose something, or make someone unhappy.

Because Jesus was fully human and shared our flesh, he was also tempted to find significance in the wrong places. But, unlike us, Jesus knew his significance went way beyond what he did, what he had, and what people thought of him. He knew exactly who he was and why he was here. Jesus shows us how to deal with these struggles.

Identity and Action

Jesus was tempted to find his identity in the same ways we are. Literally tempted—by the devil himself. It happened immediately after his baptism.

Satan was trying to steal Jesus' joy by breaking his connection with the Father. Jesus' identity was announced for all the world to hear at his baptism when he heard the Father say, "You are my Son, the Beloved; with you I am well pleased." In the presence of the Father, as one who belongs with the Father, as one rooted in joy, Jesus had a solid identity as the Son.

Jesus had a secure connection with the Father. And from this secure connection Jesus could make a significant contribution. As the Son who belongs with the Father, Jesus could pour out the blessings of God. Because he always had access to the Father's presence, Jesus could go out and fulfill the Father's purposes.

Jesus is fulfilling the identity given to Adam and Eve. They—and all of humanity—were made to dwell in God's presence and to bless the world with God's purposes. They were given a secure connection from which they could offer a significant contribution. But when temptation came, they couldn't hold onto their true identity. Sin and shame stole it from them.

Seeking to Steal Joy

This is why Jesus is tempted after his baptism. Just like Adam and Eve, and just like Israel, Jesus is tempted to turn away from his true identity as God's image. Like all of us, he is tempted to find security and significance in something else other than God's presence and purposes.

Jesus is tempted to find his significance in either what he does, what he has, or what people think of him. Satan is seeking to steal Jesus' joy by destroying Jesus' connection to the Father.

Satan is attacking Jesus' identity when, before each temptation, he says, "If you are the Son of God . . ." When Satan offers Jesus the opportunity to prove himself by performing a miracle (by turning stones to bread), Jesus refuses the identity of being *what you do*. When Satan offers Jesus all the kingdoms of the world, Jesus passes on the offer because he already has the love of the Father. Jesus refuses the identity of being *what you have*. When Satan invites Jesus to throw himself off the temple and let the angels catch him in front of the crowds, Jesus clings to the reality that he already knows his Father takes great delight in him. He refuses the identity of being *what people think of him*.

Jesus refuses to find his identity in what he can do, what he has, or what people think of him. Instead, he continually resists these temptations by living into the words spoken over him at his baptism as his source of joy. He knows he is the Son of God, so he doesn't need any of Satan's tricks to confirm that identity. He allows his identity to guide his actions, his presence with the Father to direct his purposes in the world.

If we're honest, though, this is hard to do.

Comparing Résumés

I (Geoff) am naturally competitive. Everywhere I go I constantly compare what I'm doing with what everyone else is doing, and then I want to do it better. Can I find the shortest checkout line? Can I find the quickest way home? Can I beat Cyd at this board game?

My competitiveness creates a lot of comparisons, particularly with other people. Have I lost as much hair as that guy? Have I gained as much weight as that other guy? Can I play basketball a little better than the other out-of-shape, middle-aged slightly balding guy?

Sadly, I do this with my career as well. While I was working on my doctorate, I would obsessively compare my résumé with other students'. What grades are they getting? Have they presented any academic papers at a conference? Was it a big, national conference or just a dumpy, local conference? How many peer-reviewed articles have they published? If I wasn't coming out on top, I would offer excuses for my lesser performance. "She's not pastoring at the same time. They don't have kids. He has more time." I would compare how I was doing as a pastor compared to other pastors and their churches.

In all my comparing I had reversed the relationship between identity and action. I was trying to validate my significance through all these actions (being a professor, a pastor, a father, a husband, a friend) so that I would feel good about my identity. But all of this comparison leads only to lies or despair. I either lie to myself about how great I'm doing or I despair about how awful I'm doing. Neither is a good way to live.

The battle for me is to remind myself that I'm already a child of the Father, that I already have access to love and joy. I don't need to earn my acceptance. I need to keep living into my baptism and receiving the words of the Father. I need to remember that from this place of belonging I am called to bless those around me through all my roles. My action needs to flow from my identity rather than my identity coming from my actions.

And Jesus shows us how to do this. He never confused his identity and his action. He never compared himself to others, trying to prove himself or find approval. He only acted *from* his secure identity; he never acted *to* secure his identity. And from this identity based in belonging, Jesus ventured out to do the work of blessing the world.

Blessing a Broken World

What actions come from Jesus' identity? What purpose flows from the Father's presence? The Gospel of Luke gives us a concise statement of Jesus' purpose. Just after his time of temptation, Jesus was teaching in a synagogue and he read this prophecy from the book of Isaiah.

> The Spirit of the Lord is upon me,
>> because he has anointed me
>>> to bring good news to the poor.
> He has sent me to proclaim release to the captives
>> and recovery of sight to the blind,
>>> to let the oppressed go free,
> to proclaim the year of the Lord's favor. (Luke 4:18-19)

After reading this Jesus sits down and says, "Today this scripture has been fulfilled in your hearing" (v. 21). That's a bold statement to say of yourself!

Jesus is making clear what his purpose is. He has come to bring blessing back to all people. And he will bring blessing into a broken world the way God has always done it: through the unwanted, the wandering, and the waiting. Through the poor and oppressed. Through the captives and prisoners, the blind and the lame. This is how God's kingdom comes: when those locked in sin and shame receive the joy of God's presence—the presence of the one who is glad to be with them.

Occupation and Vocation

There's a difference between how we make a living and what we live to do. How we make a living is our occupation; what we live to do is our vocation.

An *occupation* is the job we hold, the thing we get paid to do, or the particular expertise we put on a résumé. It's a position we've held, a job description we've carried out. A *vocation* is the thing we do wherever we are. It's the piece of God's blessing for the world that flows through us.

Before sin and shame took over, occupation and vocation were the same thing. We were created for the purpose of extending the blessing of God's presence in the world.

Adam and Eve's work flowed from their identity. Whenever Adam and Eve asked, Who am I? the answer was, I am God's beloved. He is pleased with me. And in their state as beloved children of the Father, they were also given the authority to be co-creators with God, to speak words of identity, to name the animals, to be tenders of life, cultivating all things to bear fruit. Their occupation and their vocation were one and the same.

But after the fall, occupations and vocations became distinct. The curse included "By the sweat of your face you shall eat bread" (Genesis 3:19). Our occupations can feel like mere toil, cursed drudgery, meaningless, and separated from God's purposes. But that doesn't mean we've lost our vocation. Jesus not only restores our humanity, he also restores our vocation.

My (Cyd's) occupation was raising small children. It described what filled my space and time. It was the work right in front of me even if I didn't get paid for it. But my vocation went beyond my occupation. I couldn't always see it, but my vocation was the same then as it is now: to help people discover who they are and to equip and encourage them to find their unique place in the family business. It doesn't matter if the people I'm called to are two tiny toddlers or world leaders—the fact is that my identity as a child of God guides my action wherever I am. I always carry the same vocation, the same piece of the Father's heart and the kingdom business.

Regardless of what I do for a living, I am always a conduit of God's blessing. This is what I live to do.

I am always an image of the rule and reign of God. I am always oriented toward the life of God. Everywhere I go, everything I do is an opportunity to extend the kingdom of God in the specific way I have been invited to do that, whether in a children's playroom, in a school classroom, a corporate boardroom, or in a full-on war zone.

The Family Business

Until you embrace God's presence and join his purpose, you will be missing something. You will feel like someone else owns your life. You will wonder if what you do matters. You will keep trying to find significance in what you do, what you have, and what people think of you. And in the long run, finding significance that way is always a prison. It's a battle you can never win.

When we find ourselves asking the questions *Do I matter? Is my work significant?* we must remember we are beloved children, just like Jesus. And just like Jesus our action must flow from our identity. We are not just accountants, students, Uber drivers, machine operators, nurses, engineers, teachers, electricians. Those are our actions, our occupations. We *are* children of God—conduits of God's blessing, proclaimers of good news, extensions of God's rule and reign, co-contributors in the family business.

What can be more significant than proclaiming the good news, participating in setting captives free, inviting all who are waiting, wandering, and unwanted into the welcome of the kingdom of God? What can be more significant than connecting people to God, who wants to be with them? What can be more meaningful than drawing people to God, who wants to bless them and bless the world through them?

Even if you're working at a job you hate, you still carry the greatest purpose the world has ever known! If you're a student, unemployed, or retired, you still carry the same mission that Jesus carried! One thing is sure. You are made to help others flourish wherever you go! You may work at a job to make a living, but let the Father's family business be what you live to do.

Living the purposes of God is the joy of *God through us.*

Practice: Seeking Vocation

Return to your joy place. Experience it again as if it were the first time you had ever been there. What stands out to you that maybe you didn't notice before? Thank God again for this special place. Ask him to make you aware of his presence with you in this place. Once you're connected with him, ask what he might like you to know about your vocation—the part in the family business that he's given you to do.

Reflection

What kinds of jobs have you had in your life?

How might God be inviting you to help others flourish in your current occupation?

Song

As you listen to "Chain Breaker" by Zach Williams, ask which part of Jesus' mission needs to flow through your life right now.

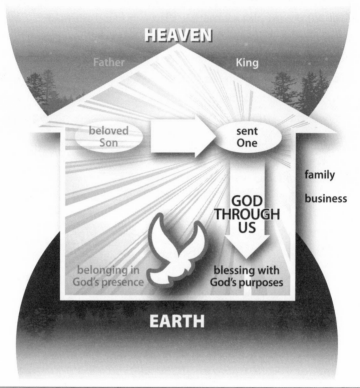

As the sent one, Jesus extends the family business of blessing the world according to his purposes.

Chapter Thirteen

Is This the Death of Me?

*O*ne stormy night our family was sitting in our living room playing a board game when there was a sudden banging on the window. Geoff leaped up and pulled back the curtain—and outside the window was our oldest chicken, a Buff Orpington named Lucy. She was squawking frantically and flapping her wings as if screaming at us for help. I (Cyd) grabbed my boots and ran into the backyard while Geoff tried to catch Lucy in the front yard to return her to the coop.

The chicken coop was in chaos. All the hens were out of their pen and squawking madly. When I opened the door and shined the flashlight in, I found a snow white hen covered in blood. She was already dead. The feathers of another hen were all over the place. We never found her. To this day, we're still not entirely sure what predator had come in. But it wasn't the first time this had happened.

Our first batch of chickens lived peacefully in a small coop with a four foot square run for several months. But they looked curious about the world beyond the fence. They seemed to want more space. So we built a fence around half our back yard so they could roam more freely. We hadn't yet realized just how many predators were eager to have easy meat wandering around.

One day I went out to get eggs and there were feathers everywhere. Four hens were missing. I found one wandering the church property, one in a tree nearby, and one was found by a neighbor whose daughter found the hen wandering the park across the street! The fourth I found in the wood pile, mostly eaten. It was a sad day.

After this incident I put a stronger lock on the coop—unsure of whether the chickens had pushed the door open on their own or if a predator had managed to get the door open.

The next summer we added more chicks to the flock, but we lost two more hens to the pair of red-tailed hawks that lived at the back of our neighbor's property. So I added an aviary net over the entire area. Then two opossums started getting into the coop somehow and helping themselves to the eggs. Then something else got in and killed another chicken.

I was pretty discouraged. After four years and constant improvements, it seemed that no matter what I did to protect the hens, the predators were still finding their way in, still helping themselves. I kept telling myself this was just the cycle of life and I shouldn't feel so bad about losing a chicken every now and then. But at the same time I felt responsible. I volunteered to care for these animals. I raised them from chicks, fed them, and cared for them. But I couldn't protect them. No matter what I did to keep them safe I couldn't do anything to keep the predators from finding their way in. The chickens were always dying and I couldn't do anything about it.

Do you ever feel this way about sin? It always seems to come back, to sneak in, to catch us off guard and overcome our defenses. No matter what we do, sin is always crouching at the door waiting to attack, waiting to kill us. Sin and death catch us by surprise, and we feel absolutely powerless against it. What is God doing about it?

What About Sin and Death?

Some of you might have been wondering, *All this talk about God's presence and purpose is well and good. All this stuff about belonging and blessing is nice. But what about sin? Sin, and the death that results, is real. Doesn't God need to deal with it?*

These are good questions. Yes, Jesus lives to bring us God's presence and purposes. Yes, Jesus comes offering belonging and blessing.

But how do we hold on to these when we are stuck in sin? How do we receive good gifts when we are weighed down by sin and shame? Adam and Eve and all of Israel couldn't keep from falling into sin and death—so what hope is there for us? What is God going to do?

How can we cross over to abundant life from the dreadful death we live in every day?

How do we cross the chasm between our life here and the fullness of Jesus' life there?

The Romans Road

Some look to what is called the Romans Road to understand how we cross this chasm between life and death. The Romans Road has three major turns in it, represented by three verses.

All have sinned and fall short of the glory of God. (Romans 3:23)

The wages of sin is death, but the free gift of God is eternal life in Christ Jesus our Lord. (Romans 6:23)

If you confess with your lips that Jesus is Lord and believe in your heart that God raised him from the dead, you will be saved. (Romans 10:9)

The argument of these verses can be summarized like this.

- All people are sinners.
- All sinners earn death.
- Therefore, all people earn death.

That's bad news! But the good news, we are told, is this.

- Instead of the wages of death, God is giving the gift of life.
- This gift is received through belief.
- Therefore, believe and you will receive life.

If we believe in Jesus, then we cross over from death to life. And this life is usually thought of as eternal life in heaven with God, avoiding the final judgment of death. All of which will occur sometime in the future.

There is much that is right in this understanding of salvation. Faith is absolutely essential to receiving the gift of salvation and to overcoming the toxic messages of shame. We must believe that Jesus—and only Jesus—is enough, that through Jesus death has been put to death.

But there is also much it leaves out.

The problem with the Romans Road is kind of like when you go to the grocery store and realize you forgot your list, so you pick up things from memory. But when you get home and start cooking, you realize you forgot some important items. The meal gets cooked, but it doesn't taste very good. That's how it is with the Romans Road. The problem is that its view of sin and death is too narrow, and salvation is too often focused solely on the future.

When it comes to sin, our problem is not just that all have committed individual sins and that all those particular sins will receive a punishment. Our problem is actually much bigger than that, going all the way back to the sin of Adam and Eve.

The Reign of Death

We don't just need salvation from our individual sins. We need salvation from all the sins coming at us from everywhere else too. We all live within webs of sin that hold us back and tie us down. This is what happened to Israel: she got caught up in the sins of the nations. We all live under a hostile power seeking to destroy us. The apostle Paul calls this hostile power the "reign of death."

Paul summarizes it like this:

> If, by the trespass of the one man, *death reigned* through that one man, how much more will those who receive God's abundant provision of grace and of the gift of righteousness *reign in life* through the one man, Jesus Christ. . . .

Just as sin *reigned in death*, so also grace might *reign through righteousness to bring eternal life* through Jesus Christ our Lord. (Romans 5:17, 21 NIV, emphasis added)

When humanity turned from God, the source of all life—not just biological life but all relational and spiritual life—then humanity entered the reign, kingdom, or realm of death. We saw this when Adam and Eve turned from God, and we saw it again when Israel turned from God. The reign of death is like all those predators getting at our chickens, even when we tried so hard to keep them out.

What does it mean for death to reign? What does it mean that death has a kingdom?

Think of your bedroom when you were a kid, when you or a sibling would put a sign on the door saying that no one could enter. You were declaring that this room is your place, your kingdom. And you are in charge of your kingdom. As a kid, your room is your realm and you reign within it.

Or think about when we get a driver's license. With a license you have entered into the realm of the public road system, and you have to obey its rules. If you don't, you'll get a ticket—or worse. This is what it means that death reigns—death has a place where it's in charge.

Because of sin, death began to reign over us. Death runs the show and forces its will on humanity. We all live inside the reign of death—not just physically but relationally and spiritually.

Living in Death

Living under the reign of death means three things.

First, living in the reign of death means we have *no place*. We have no place to belong, no place of acceptance, no place for being truly known. At its worst it is total rejection all of the time, without a home, and without a family. It is the total absence of belonging with God. It is the absence of God's presence.

Second, living in the reign of death means we have *no purpose*. It is living without significance, where everything is futile and meaningless. You constantly try to prove yourself, to prove you are needed and important, that you are worthy of love and respect and a place to belong. Living without purpose is to live without blessing others.

Last, living in the reign of death means living *under penalty*. We all live under the penalty of what we have done. We have earned our guilt and shame through our own actions. Most of us also live with the penalty of what has been done to us against our will. Either way we all live under the penalty of sin—the reign of death that we have chosen and that we had chosen for us.

Living without a place, without a purpose, and under penalty keeps us from all the benefits Jesus longs to give to us, the gift of *God with us* (place), *God through us* (purpose), and freedom from sin and shame.

Death, Sin, and Shame

The reign of death is physical, relational, and spiritual. We can think of it as the constant state of disconnection caused by sin and shame. When we are under the reign of death, we are disconnected from our true identity as those who belong in God's presence and can bless others in line with God's purposes.

When we live from this disconnected state of sin and shame, we fall into believing that we are what we do, what we have, and what people think of us. Living in the reign of death, out of a place of shame, causes us to strive after our identity and significance through empty relationships, vain accomplishments, or through keeping up appearances. The reign of death constantly tells us lies about who we are. "You're not doing enough. You're not good enough. You're doing it wrong. Nothing you do matters. You're insignificant. You don't have enough. You need more. Someone is holding you back. You deserve better. People don't respect you. If people knew, they wouldn't love you."

Like Adam and Eve listening to the serpent, these lies lead us into doubting ourselves, doubting our connections to God and to one another, and lead us straight into the shame of feeling too much, not enough. Shame leads to sin. And sin gives birth to shame. And it all leads us to hide and withdraw and retreat deeper into our false identities and fight harder to protect what we have built to keep us safe.

All this is the reign of death.

What Is God Going to Do?

Without a place to belong, without a purpose to bless others from, and under penalty, what is God going to do?

God had two options. But one of them stinks for us.

The *first option* is that God could destroy the reign of death. With a flick of his finger God could say goodbye to this reign of death and everything in it. Of course, all of us are inside the reign of death. So God would be destroying us and all of his creation. This certainly would display God's mighty power. And it would be within God's rights. God would be acting as a God of power. But would God be acting as a God of love?

The *second option* is that God could enter into this reign of death, free everyone captured inside it, and then destroy death from the inside out. With this option God eventually destroys death, but not with everyone inside it. Of course, this second option is more difficult and costly for God. It means sending the Son into the world to die, to die inside the reign of death. But this second way would also demonstrate that God is a God of love.

Because God longs for no one to perish and for all to be restored to the reign of life, God determined to save the world through love instead of through raw power.

"For the joy set before him," Jesus, the Son, entered the reign of death to do the kingdom work of the Father—to restore the reign of life, the reign of love (Hebrews 12:2 NIV).

Jesus Enters the Reign of Death

Jesus was born into this reign of death. His birth was accompanied by the slaughter of all the newborn boys in Bethlehem because Herod was trying to kill the infant King that the wise men came to see. Jesus was born into a land occupied by Roman soldiers, a violent foreign power.

Jesus ministered in this reign of death. He was tempted by the devil and confronted by evil spirits. He ministered among the sick and comforted those excluded from the community. And the human leaders—those benefiting from this reign of death—constantly opposed Jesus in all he did. In fact, they were so afraid of Jesus they finally had him killed. These leaders put Jesus to death so they could put everything back to normal.

By dying, Jesus experienced the absolute power of the reign of death. On his way to the cross Jesus was stripped naked and whipped raw. He was publicly ridiculed and shamed, hung between two criminals as if he were just another piece of trash. Jesus experienced public humiliation, the abandonment of his friends, and even the silence of God.

Jesus entered the depths of death's reign, all the way in and all the way down to the bottom of the grave—the physical grave certainly, but also the relational and spiritual grave.

Jesus Restarts the Reign of Life

But Jesus didn't die just to take our death. He died to defeat it, to overcome it, to put it to death. And how does he do that? By growing the reign of life inside the reign of death.

The apostle Paul says that death reigned because of Adam's sin. But Paul also says that through Christ a new reign, the reign of life, has begun (Romans 5:17). Jesus was so full of life—the life of the Father and the Spirit—that the power of death could not hold onto him (Acts 2:24). Death was not strong enough to keep down the Author of life.

Death thought it could kill the source of all life. Instead, Jesus took his life—his eternal life—and planted it inside death's reign, defeating it from within. When Jesus died, it was not death who won. It lost. Death died.

Because of Jesus, there is a little area of life growing inside of the reign of death. Or we could say that a little bit of heaven has come down to earth. And when God comes down to earth, life itself comes with him. And when God enters into death, life itself enters in. This life has crossed over to us; we haven't crossed over to life.

The death and life of Jesus began a slow, steady, grassroots movement to destroy death from the inside out. Death reigned because of Adam and Eve, who fell from God's presence and failed to live in God's purposes. But Jesus—fully God and fully human—entered into death and rescued us. He brings us back into God's presence and renews our partnership in God's purposes. In his life we again belong with God and can bless others with God's life. When we live in and through Jesus, we join him in this movement of bringing life to others, of bringing heaven down to earth.

This is what we need to remember most: Jesus doesn't just save us *from death*. Jesus saves us *for life*. A difference in prepositions doesn't seem to be a big deal. But in fact it changes everything.

A Shopping Cart

Our family shops at Aldi. It's a discount grocery chain. They have shopping carts, but they aren't free. You can rent a cart for a quarter, which you get back when you return the cart. So no big deal, right?

Except I (Geoff) never have the change!

So I'm at Aldi one day and I can't get a cart. I have to awkwardly wait for someone to return a cart and then beg for their quarter. It's so embarrassing. The whole point of going to Aldi is to get the groceries, and now I'm stuck just trying to get a cart.

Sometimes we can think that Jesus saving us *from death* is like Jesus saving us from not having a shopping cart. Just being saved from death is like being saved from standing around the Aldi parking lot looking for a quarter.

Many of us—spiritually—are just standing around the parking lot of life thankful that Jesus paid for our shopping cart. And we're standing around because we believe that all the good groceries from the store are only going to come in the afterlife.

But this is totally wrong! Jesus didn't die to give us an empty shopping cart that won't be filled until he comes again. Jesus has brought the reign of life to us right now, within the reign of death. Jesus' death has paid for everything in the grocery store, and we're invited to come in. The reign of life is inside the store. We just need to go in and take it off the shelves and into our bodies to let it feed us. We need to go in and start living.

We aren't supposed to wander the parking lot, hungry and longing for the good life to come when we get to heaven. Jesus has brought heaven—life, God's presence—to us. He has thrown the doors of the store wide open and has paid the bill for everything in it. It's all ours! Now! Everything we need to be nourished and whole—a place to belong, a purpose for living, freedom from penalty—already ours. Jesus bridged the gap and brought us life here, now.

Instead of us being the ones who cross over the bridge to God in heaven, Jesus crossed the bridge, bringing heaven to us now, today. Jesus didn't merely save us *from death*. He saved us *for life*.

Everything in the store has been paid for! Let's start living.

For most of this book we've assumed that you already believe in Jesus in some way—that you've already been saved from sin and death and you've got a shopping cart.

But maybe you haven't. Or maybe your faith has grown stale. Maybe it's never seemed like good news before. Maybe you've heard so much about sin that you've stopped wanting to move toward a God who seems to despise you.

But life is available to you right now, wherever you are. If you've never asked God to be with you and if you've never responded to his invitation to come into his presence, take a moment right now to let him know that's what you want to do. He's been waiting to be with you for your whole life. There's no need to delay even a moment more. Jesus put all the sin and death to death, and you don't have to carry it with you anymore.

Or maybe you've been wandering the parking lot, hungry, longing for eternity when you'll finally get to live. Maybe today is your day to say yes to all of the life that you've been saved to. Maybe today is the day you choose to fully enter the joy of Jesus and start living!

The Joy Before Him

Jesus did all of this for the sake of joy. "For the joy set before him he endured the cross, scorning its shame" (Hebrews 12:2 NIV). Just what is this joy? Remember that joy comes from being in the presence of someone who is glad to be with you. If Jesus is filled with joy at the prospect of his death, it's because he knows that his death will make it possible for God and humanity to be with one another. Jesus has the joy of bringing life where there was only death.

Does this sound like a God who doesn't like me? Does this sound like a God who is putting up with me? A God who is just tolerating my presence?

Or does this sound like a God who is doing everything possible to be with me? Who is overcoming every obstacle to our separation? Who delights in my presence and longs to bring me life?

God wants to be with you. Jesus' joy is in knowing he was restoring our place of belonging and bringing us back into the presence of God. Jesus knew he was restoring our significance and inviting us back into the purpose of God. And this gave him immeasurable *joy*, more than enough to endure the cross.

God delights in you. Because of Jesus, we are beloved children of the Father, ambassadors of the good and loving King. This identity is bestowed upon us not because of what we do, what we have, or what people think of us, but because of who God is and who God is making us to be in Jesus.

Practice: Palms Up, Palms Down

Spend some time considering the ways you have chosen the reign of death. As you confess these, turn your palms down as a way of refusing to participate any longer. Turn your palms up and receive the gifts of God with us, God through us, and freedom from sin and shame. Talk to God about your struggle to let go of the reign of death and to trust and believe the reign of life in Christ.

Reflection

What has it felt like to trust in Jesus at different times in your life? How has Jesus brought you new life? How has he released you from sin and death?

Be specific and tell him how grateful you are for all that he did so that you might live.

Song

As you listen to "Even Me" by I AM THEY, reflect on how Jesus' love and life are *for* you.

Jesus chooses to enter the domain of death in order to bring new life to all of humanity.

Part Four

God's
Movement

Chapter Fourteen

Will I Ever Learn?

*W*hen I (Cyd) was five, my mom remarried. My new dad and I had a pretty rocky relationship when I was a kid. As an adult I have a lot of compassion for where he was coming from. I don't think he ever had the experience of feeling deeply connected to someone who was glad to be with him when he was young. His father was abusive, and he grew up with a shame-saturated self-image. Lacking joy, he could only parent out of fear and anger, fiercely protecting his wounded heart. He tried to be a good dad, but because his own father had never taken delight in him or spoken words of kindness to him, he wasn't capable of speaking words of delight and kindness to me. Instead, he spoke out of the identity that his abusive father had given him.

How could you be so stupid?

You'll never learn.

How many times do I have to tell you . . . ?

Do you ever think before you do things?

You're so sensitive. You better toughen up or you're not going to make it in the real world.

I lived my life in reaction to those words. I alternated between defying them and giving in to them. I vacillated between proving how wrong they were and believing I was stupid.

The Struggle to Change

Words have power. In the beginning God created the heavens and the earth by speaking. There was nothing; God spoke, and then there was everything. Words are creational, formational. On the flip side, words can be terribly destructive. They have the power to warp our identities and wither our purposes, destroying life and obliterating hope. With just a few words the serpent introduced Adam and Eve—and all of humanity—to the captivity of shame and sin.

I grew up in a great church, surrounded by wonderful people who were like family to me, celebrating my achievements and sharing my sadnesses. I knew I was loved by this community, and I knew the people there were pulling for me. In middle school I publicly declared my faith with great joy in front of this congregation—believing that God had called me to good and beautiful things and that he was shaping and forming my life.

But the words from my dad always replayed in the back of my mind. Like a poison they nibbled at the edges of the good and beautiful things. No matter how many good things were happening around me, no matter how brilliant the circumstances of my life were, I assumed that things would fall apart at any moment. And of course I assumed it would be my fault. It was always my fault because I was stupid, I wasn't thinking, I would never learn.

Like many of us, I developed some unhealthy coping mechanisms to try to numb my pain and shame. I had codependent friendships, unhealthy romantic relationships, self-destructive personal habits. By the time I was finishing college, I wanted to leave everything and everyone behind. I hoped that a change of environment would jump-start a new reality for me, to get me out of all my destructive coping patterns. And so, without knowing a soul, I moved to California.

But my old life followed me there. After a painful year of even deeper messes, I fell into a community of people who talked about Jesus as if he was real, like they actually knew him. I wanted what they had.

I determined to rekindle my faith and live for Jesus again. This time I was sure it would be different. It was a different community—one full of grace, forgiveness, understanding—and I was going to stick with it this time. Things went well for over a year. I thought I had overcome the old words, the ones that told me I was stupid and never learned. I thought I had overcome the old patterns that had sprung up to defend me from the painful words. I decided to move back to Michigan and live with my parents to save money for graduate school.

After only a week of living in my parents' basement, it became clear that the words hadn't gone away. I had just pushed them down in my mind where they had been a little quieter for a time. But now that I was back home, they were back too—with a vengeance! I fell back into the destructive patterns I had developed before. And all I could do was yell at myself, *Why are you so stupid? You should have known better! This is all your fault!* The poisonous words were no longer nibbling; they were threatening to devour me.

Every once in a while I would still pull out my Bible and look for some kind of hope and encouragement in the midst of my despair. I often came upon a verse that only seemed to make things worse. "Therefore, if anyone is in Christ, the new creation has come: The old has gone, the new is here!" (2 Corinthians 5:17 NIV).

Where is the new creation? I would cry out. *The old clings to me like a terrible stench. I can't wash it away, it won't fade, it never leaves me. All the forward motion I try to make is like trudging through sludge. I'm still the same old me, doing the same stupid things.*

I was thoroughly and completely discouraged, hopeless that I could ever change, despairing that I would never change. I was ready to give up on the whole Jesus thing. Shame hung thick and heavy about me, stealing my humanity and cutting me off from everyone—especially God.

I didn't know that I was expecting something that the verse wasn't promising. I was expecting radical, instantaneous change. I was probably expecting those perfect strawberries from chapter ten to appear in my life. But this verse is not a statement of experience as much as a statement of fact. Whether I feel it or not, the fact is that when anyone is in Christ, new creation comes.

When I cry out, "Jesus, save me! I need you to bring me to the Father! I want to belong to the family!" then I really am a new creation in Christ. But if this is true, why do so many lives tell a different story?

Why Didn't Jesus Stick?

We once had a next door neighbor who had gone to prison for committing multiple robberies to support his heroin addiction. While in prison he found Jesus and was radically changed. It was an incredible story! After years in prison he came home. He was baptized in our church on Easter Sunday. He got a job. He was completely immersed in church life.

But then, six weeks later, he overdosed on heroin. We were all devastated. After the funeral I (Cyd) will never forget what his dad said, "I thought he was going to be different. I guess the Jesus thing just didn't stick."

Many of us have this experience. We make a decision, we want a new life, we cry out to Jesus in desperation—"Lord, make me new!"—and we expect everything to change immediately. We hope to live in total victory. We hope never to struggle with sin again. But that doesn't happen. In fact, the struggle feels worse than ever. Life actually seems harder instead of easier.

If new creation is a fact, why is life still such a struggle? What is going on?

Life is a battle—that's what's going on!

Still in the Battle

The battle has already been won, and yet it's not completely over.

To illustrate this, people sometimes talk about World War II because it ended in stages. The decisive battle was fought on the beaches of Normandy on June 6, 1944 (D-day), but victory in Europe was not declared until almost a year later on May 8, 1945 (V-E Day). And Japan didn't officially surrender until September 2, 1945.

And even so, the war continued to drag on in the Philippines. Japanese soldiers, cut off from their central command, didn't immediately receive word that the war was over. A troop of Japanese soldiers had been defeated on the island of Lubang, but four intelligence officers survived by hiding in the jungle. They never heard about Hiroshima or Nagasaki. They never heard about the surrender of Japan. They continued to engage in guerilla warfare, believing the war was still going on.

When the United States realized that these soldiers had no way of communicating with the Japanese command, they decided to air drop leaflets, letting them know of Japan's surrender. But these soldiers saw the leaflets as the equivalent of "fake news!" They couldn't believe their government would ever surrender, so they kept on fighting.

One of the soldiers eventually gave up. Two others were killed. But one soldier, named Hiroo Onoda, continued to hold out on his own, in the jungle, continuing to cause trouble for the Filipino people. Many years later, a Japanese journalist found him and told him that the emperor was worried about him and wanted him to come home. But Onoda said he would not leave his post until he was relieved of duty by his commanding officer. The Japanese government found his commanding officer, now retired as a bookseller, and flew him to the island of Lubang to officially relieve him of duty. Onoda finally surrendered—twenty-nine years after Japan had officially surrendered. Twenty-nine years!

Spiritually and relationally, this is the current state of the world.

The Real Battle

We are in a battle. And as Paul says, it is not against flesh and blood. It's against "the rulers, against the authorities, against the cosmic powers of this present darkness, against the spiritual forces of evil in the heavenly places" that seek to enslave our hearts and minds

(Ephesians 6:12). These spiritual forces are the generals within the reign of death. But Jesus has already won this battle in his death and resurrection—definitively.

Nevertheless, the reign of death still rages on, fighting for the hearts and minds of each one of us. The reign of death keeps attacking us, telling us that we don't belong in God's presence. Telling us that we don't really have a share in God's purposes. The reign of death keeps firing false words at us, lying to us about who we are and what we are made for. A new creation has already come in Christ, but the reign of death still battles on.

In the face of these false words we must remember and believe the true words. In Christ, we *are* children of the Father who belong in the presence of God—*God with us*. In Christ, we *are* ambassadors of the King, offering blessing to all as we live in God's purposes—*God through us*.

The powers and forces of evil are still engaged in guerrilla warfare to destroy, disconnect, and distract us from all of this. The human heart is the territory of the most significant battle ever waged. The battle has already been won, but the fighting isn't over yet.

The Battleground

All of those wounded and hurting places that exist inside of us are the battleground. The reign of death plants vicious lies in those places: lies about who God is, who we are, and what life is about. In response to those lies, we make promises to ourselves. *I'll never allow myself to be hurt like that again.* We stop believing God and start fending for ourselves.

And when we do, death plants a flag and claims some territory. Every part of us that the enemy claims is a place where we cannot return to joy. It's a place of disconnection and shame—a place where we've told God we don't need him or can't be with him. We wall ourselves off from being connected with him or with anybody else in that place.

What happened to Adam and Eve happens to us. The serpent asked questions to sow seeds of *doubt*. On top of these he poured the water of lies to deepen the *distress*. And from all this distress came the sense that Adam and Eve were *deficient* and *defective*. Adam and Eve believed these wrong words about themselves and about God. And these words crept into their hearts and caused them to die in sin and in shame.

The human heart and mind is still the battleground. The only way to live the new life in Christ is to experience healing at our core—in our hearts and our minds—to replace old identities with new ones.

To do this we must replace the old words of death with the new words of life. Remember the words the Father spoke over Jesus at his baptism? Those words were the source of Jesus' joy, and they can be the source of ours as well.

Living in Christ

If new creation is a fact, then we can live as if it's actually true. This isn't wishful thinking; it's hopeful determination. It's persistent faith— resisting the lies and insisting on the truth.

Because we are in Christ, we are beloved by the Father and full of the Holy Spirit. It's a fact. We must listen carefully for the song of joy, tuning our ears to hear the God who is always glad to be with us. Only then can we attune our hearts to the song of joy.

Living in Christ means two enormous things.

First, we belong with God. And as a mark of that belonging, the Holy Spirit fills us just like he descended on Jesus at his baptism. It is by the Spirit of the Son that we cry, "Abba! Father!" (Galatians 4:6). We are loved as completely and fully as Jesus is loved by his Father, who takes as much delight in us as he does in his own Son.

Living in Christ means God wants to be *with us* as much as he wants to be with his own Son.

Second, living in Christ means we can again live for the purposes of God. We are sent on mission just as Jesus was sent. God, the King of all the universe, sent his Son with clear instructions to extend the rule and reign of the kingdom into all places so life might flourish everywhere. And the Holy Spirit filled Jesus with all the strength and power he needed to be faithful to this mission. Everything we see Jesus doing is what his Father is doing. In Christ we are swept up into that same calling, that same vocation, and that same Spirit—that same Spirit that raised Jesus from the grave. And because we know we are beloved, the always wanted ones, we can extend that joy to the waiting, the wandering, and the unwanted.

Living in Christ means God wants to work *through us* as much as he is already working through his own Son.

In Christ we know who we are and why we matter. We belong to the Father, and by the power of the Holy Spirit we bring the Father's blessing to the entire world. We have access to God's presence and are invited to join God's purposes. We are connected to God and have a meaningful contribution to make to the world. In Christ, by his Spirit, God is with us and we are with God.

These are the facts.

But knowing the facts and living the facts are two different things.

Old and New Words

When I (Cyd) was first called into pastoring in my thirties, all the old, painful words from my childhood came back to haunt me. As many times as I had heard Jesus tell me directly that he loves me, I still had the sense that I was going to make a horrible mess of things. After all, the words I most believed about myself were that *I don't think, I'm stupid,* and *I never learn.*

So I decided to ask Jesus about these words, and he met me in prayer in a radically life-changing way. He brought to mind his baptism, but I was there with him. I stood with him in the Jordan River, looking up as the heavens split open, feeling the weight of the Spirit come upon me. But most of all I heard the words of my Father, "You are beloved. With you, I am well pleased." With these words spoken over me—as much as over Jesus—I heard Jesus say to me, "I trust you. Let's go."

In Jesus we can all hear the words of the Father, saying, "You are beloved. With you, I am well pleased." In Jesus we all receive the Holy Spirit, descending upon us.

I find that even now, every time I'm about to push into some new territory or take a new risk for the sake of the kingdom of God, the old, dead words start nibbling at me again. At that point I can either let the old words live, or I can remember that the same Holy Spirit who empowered Christ to overcome the temptation of the enemy gives me the power to fight for new creation. I can either live from the old words, or I can believe the words of my baptism, that in Christ the Father says over me, "You are my daughter. With you, I am well pleased." Faith is a matter of choosing which words we live by.

Remembering and believing those new words change everything!

Those words have the power to heal and transform. They bring me out of my distress and back to joy. They remind me that I am always wanted, that I always belong.

Because in Christ God is always glad to be with me and is always for me, I am never invisible, unknown, misunderstood, shamed, cast out, or abandoned. I am not stupid or unthinking or incapable of learning. Rather, because the Holy Spirit is with me, I am seen. I am known. I am understood. I am capable. Like Hagar, God hears me in my distress and meets me there with gladness. I am understood, loved fiercely and deeply. And God, my Father and King who is always *with me*, is also always *for me*, and trusts me enough to work *through me*, giving me the courage to face any situation.

Practice: Living in Christ

Go to your joy place again. Receive the gift of this place, paying attention to details and delighting in being here. Ask God to show you how he is with you in this place. Ask him to remind you of the true words that he speaks over you in Christ. Allow them to soak in. Open your palms to receive all these words of life. As you notice resistance rising, turn your palms down as a way of choosing to ignore words that bring death.

Reflection

Take some time to consider the words you choose to live by. What are the messages that replay in your head as you go about your life?

Who spoke those words to you?

Consider what it might look like to have compassion on the person who said those things and to stand with Jesus as he says, "Father, forgive them; for they do not know what they are doing."

Song

Listen to "Live Like You're Loved" by Hawk Nelson. What would it take for you to believe and live like you're loved?

All who trust Jesus (living in Christ) are a new creation, the people where heaven and earth overlap.

Chapter Fifteen

Will I Ever Find Peace?

*G*rowing up, my (Geoff's) twin brother and I would often punch each other—especially through our teenage years. Sometimes playfully, oftentimes not. We punched each other for any and every reason, great or small. Usually, the punching came after some verbal sparring that escalated into personal insults. Then came a love tap on the shoulder. This was reciprocated by a stronger punch. On it would go until someone was crying—or at least tearing up—because the jab was a little too strong, a little more vicious than intended. Then the offender would apologize. The instigator reciprocated. And we'd get back to whatever we were doing. At home, at school, at church, in a car, this would happen over and over, like the rising and the setting of the sun.

It's not just brothers who do this. Day in and day out, in the office, on social media, and in our families—we pick on each other. We nitpick about dumb things and important things. We argue over money, politics, and religion; parking spots, promotions, and parties.

On the surface all this fighting looks like attacking, but it's really defending. More often than not we fight to protect ourselves. We protect ourselves from feeling embarrassed, stupid, incompetent, left out, or forgotten. We fight to protect the walls we've raised around our hearts and our minds in response to the wounds we've experienced.

We fight to protect our sense of belonging, and we fight to protect our sense of purpose in the world.

Will this fighting ever end? Will we ever stop picking on each other in big and small ways? Will we ever stop feeling the need to protect ourselves and our territory and finally find peace?

The good news is that as new creations in Christ, we are being built into the place of God's presence (*God with us*). When we live in Christ we no longer need to build walls that keep us safe. Instead, we are being built into God's place of peace.

The Place(s) of God's Presence

First, God built his home with humanity in the Garden with Adam and Eve. Then he moved into the tabernacle/temple. He came even closer in the person—the flesh—of Jesus Christ. And then, on the day of Pentecost, Jesus fulfills his promise of his forever presence (Acts 2).

Just as each place of God's presence was filled with God's glory, the Spirit of God comes again to earth—this time to fill all those who are in Christ. A violent wind blows and tongues of fire come down on the followers of Jesus to show that God's presence now rests on the church. The filling of the Spirit marks the church as the new place of God's presence. All those living in Christ are now where heaven and earth meet.

It's no wonder the apostle Paul says we are a "holy temple in the Lord . . . being built together to become a dwelling in which God lives by his Spirit" (Ephesians 2:21-22 NIV).

But what does that mean?

And how does it solve all the fighting?

A Place for Peace

To understand what it means to be built together as God's temple—and why it matters for all our fighting—we need to go back to Jesus and his criticism of the temple in Jerusalem.

Just before his trial and execution Jesus expressed his anger at how God's temple was being used.

On reaching Jerusalem Jesus entered the temple courts and began driving out those who were buying and selling animals for sacrifices. He overturned their tables and would not allow anyone to carry merchandise through the temple courts. And while doing this he exclaimed,

Is it not written:

"My house will be called a house of prayer for all nations"?

But you have made it a den of robbers. (Mark 11:15-17)

Let's not get too distracted by all the drama—overturning tables and driving out the livestock. We need to focus on the reason Jesus took this drastic step against the temple—one which led directly to his death because the people in charge were so deeply threatened by it.

At that time the temple had different courtyards for different people. In the inner courts, Jewish men and women could come closest to where the priests worked. But the Gentiles—everyone not Jewish—had to stay in the outer court. The merchants and money changers, the coins and the cows, were most certainly in this outer court, where the Gentiles had to stay if they wanted to pray to God. This outer court was the closest they could come to God's presence in the temple.

In clearing out the merchants and money changers Jesus was making room for the Gentiles to pray and seek God's presence in peace. Quoting Isaiah 56:7, Jesus reminds everyone that God's temple is meant to be a house of prayer for all people, not just the Jewish people. In other words, God's presence was meant to be a blessing for everyone. The Jews were disrupting Gentiles' access to God, making the temple a place of division and fighting instead of a place of life and blessing for all.

The Dividing Wall

At Jesus' time there had never been a bigger dividing wall than the one between Jews and Gentiles. The Jews had God's law and felt secure inside the walls of its commands. And the Gentiles—who were excluded by the law—were angry about it.

The Jews were like those of us who read the letter of God's law and make it into rules and religion, building a wall separating us from "those" people. We smugly look down on others for not sharing our views and opinions, criticizing their stupidity and ignorance.

And the Gentiles were like those of us who feel excluded by the church, snubbed and rejected for not fitting into the plan or program. Or maybe you prefer being on the outside, living as a rebel, pushing the limits of what people say you can or can't do, fighting with all those fools who have sold out to the system.

The wall between Jews and Gentiles is an echo of how we all build walls to protect ourselves and to separate ourselves from other people. We build walls around the sports teams we root for, the political policies we stand for, and the companies we work for. We build walls to separate us from the people we are against, the policies we fear, and everything else that is wrong in the world. We build walls around our pain and our failures, making sure that someone else is to blame.

Breaking Down the Wall

Thinking about all the walls we build, and especially the one between Jews and Gentiles, the apostle Paul said this about Jesus:

> [Jesus] is our peace; in his flesh he has made both groups into one and has broken down the dividing wall, that is, the hostility between us. He has abolished the law with its commandments and ordinances, that he might create in himself one new humanity in place of the two, thus making peace. (Ephesians 2:14-15)

In his body, Jesus is making peace by tearing down the walls dividing us. Jesus is tearing down all the things that make us fight with each other—our views on politics, religion, and culture; our views on education, income equality, or marital status; even our views on how long before the grass needs to be cut in our neighbor's yard, how loud they should play their music on the weekend, and how rowdy their kids are when they come over.

All the things we fight over, big or little, are being torn down by Jesus and replaced by a "dwelling in which God lives by his Spirit" (Ephesians 2:22 NIV). What does it mean to be built into a dwelling place for God?

We've seen already that the place where God dwells is the place where heaven and earth overlap. Now, instead of finding God in the Garden, in the tabernacle or temple, or in the person of Jesus, we find God in all the followers of Jesus. Through him we have "access in one Spirit to the Father" (Ephesians 2:18).

Special Access

One summer day our family went to a Chicago Cubs baseball game. The family sitting in front of us turned out to be season-ticket holders. They knew all the ushers, where the shortest snack lines were, and which bathrooms were the least crowded. They also knew the best way to get an autograph from the players.

During the last inning they stood up and said, "It's time." We followed them as they marched their way through to a particular gate on the lower level. Security guards were just starting to put up barriers to protect the players. The family showed us exactly where to stand. Because we had left our seats early, we were the first ones there.

They gave us tips on addressing the players only as "Mr. Bryant" or "Mr. Rizzo" and never by first names. They told us that people who shout the players' first names or are rude never get autographs. You have to be polite and considerate, patient and grateful.

As the players started to trickle out, we all got excited. Some players smiled and waved. It was fun to see the players close up, but most kept walking right on by. Some completely ignored us. Finally, Willson

Contreras, the Cubs catcher, stopped. He started taking the hats and shirts, baseballs and notebooks, and signing them. He got to the end of the gate, where our boys were, and signed both of their hats. Then he walked away.

Through the invitation of the family sitting in front of us, we were given special access and a special opportunity that others didn't get. Whether it's a famous person, a boss, a popular friend, or even just your favorite sibling, we all long for access to the people we find important.

Access to the Father

Jesus' outrage in the temple courts was about access to the presence of God. All people were supposed to have access to the outer courts—to God's presence. The Jews were allowed a little closer, but the Gentiles were still welcome to draw near.

But the Jews, in an effort to protect their own access to God's house, refused to create space for the Gentiles. We see this over and over again in both the little and the big fights that we have.

Look at American politics. Why do the political parties fight each other so ferociously to get someone into the White House? It's not for the location in Washington, DC, or the luxurious interior. It's about access to power. The president has access to all the resources of the United States. And by getting the president of their choice into the White House, political parties believe they will benefit from access to those same resources.

Access to the presence of God is what humanity has been longing for and fighting over ever since Adam and Eve lost it. Cain killed Abel because he felt less access to God and longed for his approval (Genesis 4:1-16). The people of Babel tried to storm heaven itself with their tower (Genesis 11:1-9). All of our fights are ultimately about this one thing: Do I have a place? Will I lose my place? Whether we realize it or not, we always seek access to the presence of God. We all long for the love of the Father and the trust of the King. We yearn for connection and want to make a meaningful contribution. It all comes back to the presence and purpose of God.

But we don't have to fight for something that is already ours. Remember how the new creation is already a fact for those who are in Christ? The same is true for access to the Father. In Christ the doors to God's house are flung wide open. In Christ all the resources of the kingdom of heaven are poured out to us—not for someday but for right now. Heaven and earth come together in the people of God. God is with us! And all are welcome to have access to the Father, through the peace of Jesus, who tore down all dividing walls and is building his church into the house of God by his Spirit.

Capacity in Jesus

But what good is access if we have no capacity to enjoy it? Access can be fruitless in some cases and even harmful in others. Access to a safety deposit box at the bank does us no good if we have nothing of value to put in it. Access to the sun can leave us blistered if we have tender skin. Access to drugs can lead to addiction. And access to a nuclear reactor without a protective suit is toxic.

In chapter five, when we focused on the fall of humanity and the loss of God's presence, we talked about how—because of sin and shame—humanity had lost the capacity to dwell in God's presence. Like a worn and brittle balloon, we would break if filled up with the full breath of God's Spirit. Because of sin and death, God's full presence is a threat to us. In chapter seven we talked about how, in our weakened state, God's presence is like a fire that could either burn up or bless humanity. Israel was given the tabernacle and the temple as a fireplace for God's glorious presence so God could dwell close to his people without burning them up. But Israel failed to properly maintain this fireplace of God's presence, and this too was lost. Without dramatic intervention, access to the presence of God is totally destructive to us because of our incapacity to handle it.

Before Christ, God's presence was too fierce for humanity to bear. The hold of sin and shame was too great. But Jesus entered into the reign of death and defeated sin and shame once and for all. Jesus drove out all the barriers to God's presence. In Christ we are no longer captives to sin and shame. Instead, we are part of the new creation—a new humanity. And this new humanity has the capacity to dwell in God's presence, to be filled with his Spirit. In fact, we are the place where heaven and earth come together.

But what does this have to do with peace?

Children of the Father

The best news about access to the Father is that there's an unlimited number of places. It's not like that gate at Wrigley Field where we got autographs. It's not like seats in a movie theater. It's not "while supplies last" like a Black Friday sale. There is unlimited space in the kingdom of God. God's presence is available without limitation and without restriction. And that means we don't have to fight each other. There's enough for everyone.

When we know we have a place, we don't need to protect our spot. We don't need to fight, because we have nothing to defend. We don't have to try to set ourselves apart and be noticed because God sees each of us and is glad to be with us. And the peace that comes from knowing we belong allows us to give up fighting, protecting, and defending ourselves.

We are the house of God, his temple on earth, filled with his presence by his Spirit. We are a people of peace because Jesus broke down all the walls and restored our humanity.

Remember, to be human means we are the images, the idols, of God. In Jesus we are restored to our rightful position in God's presence. We don't have to wonder about our place. Not only do we belong in God's presence but God is overjoyed that we have been restored! He has always wanted us to be with him. He enjoys being with us. We don't have to wonder if God really likes us. We can be sure!

He loves us so much that he lets us introduce him to the world. As God's image (idol) in God's temple (his people, the church), you are the tangible presence of God. And not just you but the entire church.

The church is where heaven comes to earth, where everyone has access to the presence of God. And where the Spirit of the Lord is, there is the fullness of joy. Through the people of God all are welcomed into the peace of Jesus Christ. There is no more fighting for access—only an invitation to come and see that the Lord is good.

Practice: Breath Meditation

Sit comfortably. Take a few deep breaths. Pay attention to your breathing, how air flows through your body. God breathed into Adam, and Adam became a living being. God's presence filled the temple in a cloud—which is air. Jesus breathed on his disciples and invited them to receive the Holy Spirit. At Pentecost the Spirit came upon the people in a mighty wind. Reflect on breathing and allow each breath to remind you that you have access to God who breathed life into you by his Spirit.

Reflection

Think about people in your life that you have access to—people you can call anytime. How does it feel to be around these people?

What would it be like to feel that kind of belonging and access in the presence of God?

Song

Listen to "The Gospel" by Ryan Stevenson. How can we be and proclaim the gospel to each other?

All people living in Christ—by the Spirit—are the new temple, the place of God's joyous presence.

Chapter Sixteen

Did I Really Sign Up for This?

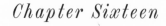

*G*eoff wanted to write this book long before I did. He's written a book before and he already thinks of himself as a writer. But I don't. Sometimes I write, but I'm not a writer. Somehow, they seem different. And there are already so many books—about the Bible, the church, spiritual life. Why does the world need another book?

But as I talked with people about the themes of this book, I saw how excited they were to hear that they belong with a God who is always glad to be with them and that they can bless the world when they join him in what he has always been doing. It seemed to be connecting with people. And it seemed that God wouldn't let the idea go, so I gave in and we started working on the book.

For the first few months everything went smoothly for us. Geoff and I had been talking about this stuff for years and it was a relief to get it out. We worked well together, and I started to wonder if maybe I actually am a writer after all. We were about half way through the book, and six months from our deadline, when God surprised us. He moved us to another state.

After being at the same church for seventeen years, and in the same house for fifteen, we were unexpectedly called away to a new church in a new city. As you might imagine, the writing stopped.

In the midst of this major life change, it was as if the book no longer existed for me. Not only did I stop writing, but I also stopped identifying as a writer. When the thought of the book crept back into my mind I would think, *I'm not a writer. I was just pretending!*

But we had signed a contract. There was a real editor waiting for the manuscript, a real publisher ready to print it, and real people—like you—ready to read it someday. It didn't matter if I didn't feel like a real writer. I had the responsibilities of a writer whether I felt like one or not.

There are times in all of our lives when we feel in over our head. When life all of a sudden gets *real*. No matter how big, hard, or heavy the task before us, it's our responsibility. In those times we often want to step back and say, "I was just kidding! I was only pretending!"

Along with all the joy that comes with being a child of God, there are also real responsibilities, real power, real battles, and real sacrifices. This realization can be overwhelming. Some days we may not feel like a child of God. Some days we might not want to be caught up in new creation coming.

But that doesn't make it any less real.

When It Gets Real

Maybe this is what the disciples experienced in their life with Jesus as well. All of a sudden it's not just Jesus who's doing the work. It's them.

In chapter fifteen we discussed how God's Spirit came upon the disciples at Pentecost. All of a sudden they became the people of God's presence—the place where heaven and earth come together. But it also means they were called into the same purposes as Jesus. They were supposed to do everything that Jesus did.

To understand this we need to look at the Gospel of Luke and the book of Acts. Together, they make one book, split into two parts. The first part is about the ministry of Jesus. The second part is about the disciples continuing Jesus' ministry. Together, Luke and Acts give us a picture of the family business that Jesus came to do.

First, Jesus proclaims his purpose:

> to bring good news to the poor. . . .
> To proclaim release to the captives,
>   and recovery of sight to the blind,
>   to let the oppressed go free,
> to proclaim the year of the Lord's favor. (Luke 4:18-19)

In the first part of Luke, this is exactly what we see Jesus doing.

As Jesus goes about the family business, he gathers disciples. After they've been with him and watched him for a while, he sends them out to do what he's doing. He tells them to go into the towns and "cure the sick who are there, and say to them, 'The kingdom of God has come near to you'" (Luke 10:9). When the disciples come back, thrilled that they could actually do what Jesus sent them to do, Jesus responds to their excitement, "See, I have given you authority . . . over all the power of the enemy. . . . But rejoice that your names are written in heaven" (Luke 10:19-20). He has given access to all of the resources of the family business, but he wants to be sure they won't forget that the whole reason they have the power is because they've been brought into the family!

After destroying the reign of death by his crucifixion and resurrection, Jesus comes to his disciples and explains that what began in Jerusalem will not stay in Jerusalem. He tells them, "I am sending upon you what my Father promised; so stay here in the city until you have been clothed with power from on high" (Luke 24:49).

But the disciples are still expecting Jesus to rule and reign from Jerusalem. After spending so much time with Jesus, they still don't quite understand the family business. Right before Jesus ascends to his Father, the disciples ask him, "Lord, is this the time when you will restore the kingdom to Israel?" (Acts 1:6).

Jesus explains that while he is going back to his Father, the family business isn't closing down. Instead, the disciples will be involved in the day-to-day work. "You will receive power when the Holy Spirit has come upon you; and you will be my witnesses in Jerusalem, in all Judea and Samaria, and to the ends of the earth" (Acts 1:8).

The whole time Jesus was doing the work of his Father, he was also preparing the disciples to continue that work after his ascension. Jesus was training them to take his place, to continue the work that he had been doing. He was training them to be human again—to be the image of God in the world, the markers of the rule and reign of the one true King.

The purpose Jesus proclaimed for himself in Luke 4 was the mission statement of the family business, which Jesus invites his friends into. On the day of Pentecost that invitation suddenly becomes real. It's no longer about watching Jesus do the work. It's no longer supervised practice. Rehearsal is over. This is the real thing.

The power and authority Jesus always claimed he had are now unleashed on and through his disciples. They finally get it. They understand that all the resources of the kingdom of heaven have been given to them. What begins in Jerusalem is meant to spread across the entire world. This was always what Jesus had in mind. Suddenly, when the Spirit comes upon them, they become fully human and are given the capacity not only to enjoy their connection with God but to make a meaningful contribution toward the mission of the family.

Remember, to be human means two things: belonging in the presence of God, and blessing the world according to God's purposes. Here we see the disciples doing both of these things as they become Spirit-filled flesh, fully human and filled with God's presence. Now they are sent to extend the rule and reign—the blessing—of the kingdom of God. They've been given the presence of God so they can participate in the purposes of God. It's their turn.

The disciples were now an outpost of God's kingdom. They were on the frontlines of the battle for God's kingdom. When people spent time with this early church community, they got an introduction to a new family, a peculiar people, a different culture.

Kingdom Outposts

To get a sense for just how different this kingdom culture is meant to be, think about neighborhoods in larger cities. Pockets of cultures in these bigger cities are so much like the countries they come from that they have names like Little Italy, Koreatown, Little Havana, Chinatown, and Little Warsaw.

When I (Cyd) lived in California, I enjoyed making trips to Chinatown in San Francisco. I loved the feeling of leaving the United States and setting foot on foreign soil without actually buying a plane ticket. Whole ducks hung in the windows and fresh bao buns steamed in wooden trays. Dried fish, herbs, and mushrooms overflowed their bowls. Everything looked, smelled, sounded, and tasted distinctly different from what was usual for me. I felt like I was in a different country.

When our family had the opportunity to go to Hong Kong, I was surprised at how familiar it felt. I recognized the ducks hanging in the windows, the smell of steaming bao, the taste of the sauces, and the sound of Cantonese being spoken. I had never been to Hong Kong before, but I had a small glimpse of what to expect because of the time I had spent in Chinatown. That little cultural outpost was a foretaste of another country.

In the same way, the early church in Jerusalem was a foretaste of the kingdom of God. But what started in Jerusalem was meant to spread across the entire earth—into all of creation. Just like Chinatown in San Francisco is an outpost of the faraway Hong Kong culture, so Jesus established an outpost of the kingdom—but one that he intended to spread throughout the whole world. What started with Jesus continued in the early church, and what started in the early church continues today.

When we put our hope and trust in Jesus, we don't merely become children in the family (God's presence); we also get brought into the family business (God's purposes).

Royal Ambassadors

Just as I had the responsibilities of a writer whether I felt like one or not, being part of the family business is a fact. It's not something we volunteer for. We are automatically included in the family business when we join the family. We are representing the family, whether we want to or not. Like the new creation, it's a fact whether we feel it or not.

Because the family business is extending the kingdom of God, this means all the children of the Father are also ambassadors of the King. The apostle Paul tells us this in 2 Corinthians 5:20—just a couple verses after he had proclaimed that all who are in Christ are a new creation. He says, "*We are therefore Christ's ambassadors*, as though God were making his appeal through us. We implore you on Christ's behalf: Be reconciled to God" (NIV, emphasis added).

We are royal ambassadors sent as official representatives with the full power and authority of the kingdom of God behind us. We represent the King. He entrusts us to do business on his behalf, to negotiate treaties, to make trade agreements. Everything we do reflects on his reputation, his good name.

We know someone who is an ambassador for an athletic clothing company. He gets free clothing and free gym memberships because his life is consistent with the brand. When people see him working out, the company wants people to notice that he wears their clothes while doing so. They want their name to be associated with his lifestyle. He's good advertising for them.

Likewise, we are image bearers. Everywhere we go, we bear the name of God. Our lifestyle influences how people think of the God who has marked us as his own. Our contribution to the family mission is meant to be a blessing to all the world.

Unfortunately, this mission can also feel pretty overwhelming.

Lip Service

I (Cyd) had a friend who didn't know Jesus but happened to get a job at a Christian organization. All over the office there were plaques that listed the mission, vision, and values of the company. Embedded in those was language about glorifying God, submitting to God's authority, and following biblical principles. Everyone who worked there identified as a Christian, except my friend.

Because I was familiar with the company and knew some people who worked there, I immediately became concerned that she would not be seen as a person but would be turned into the office project. Sure enough, after a few weeks, every member of the staff had shared the gospel with her and had pressed her for a decision for Christ. Every time, she politely declined. After each of these interactions, the person who had "failed to save her" no longer spent time with her. It was as if she wasn't worthy of any of their time or attention unless she was going to say yes to Jesus.

She shared with me how the work environment had become hostile for her. She talked about how people were not only generally rude and cold but even blamed her for things that weren't her responsibility. When she told me she was going to quit, she explained, "I can't work there anymore, and I want absolutely nothing to do with their God."

The mission, vision, and values of this company missed the point of the mission of God's family business. This company wasn't doing the hard work of being an outpost of the kingdom, living the culture of the King. Instead, they had become a checkpoint or a border crossing into the kingdom. They failed to be an aqueduct of God's full blessing. Overwhelmed by the task of reconciliation, they shrunk the work to just getting people saved.

The Family Business

The family business is all about reconciliation—about bringing people back together, bringing them back to connection, back to joy. In the same place the apostle Paul talks about us being a new creation and ambassadors in Christ, he gives us a mission statement for the family business:

All this [new creation] is from God, who reconciled us to himself through Christ, and has given *us* the ministry of reconciliation; that is, in Christ God was reconciling the world to himself, not counting their trespasses against them, and entrusting the *message of reconciliation to us.* (2 Corinthians 5:18-19, emphasis added)

Reconciliation is the process of bringing people back into relationship. Relationally, when people are at odds, they need to be reconciled. When shame has pulled people apart through fear and fighting, reconciliation brings them together again. Reconciliation moves people from shame back to joy. Sounds like a pretty great family business to be in—but not an easy one.

Unfortunately, rather than focusing on the full family business of reconciliation, too often we focus on the goal of just "saving souls"—we turn people into salvation projects. As a human being, this "project" is an image bearer of God, someone who belongs in God's presence. God longs to be with each person. What kind of message do we communicate about our God when we write people off as soon as they refuse his invitation? Didn't Adam and Eve refuse God's invitation? Didn't Israel? Didn't each of us at one time or another? But God never stopped longing for reconciliation. God never gave up on the work of bringing blessing.

We are ministers of reconciliation. That's the lifestyle we're called to as followers of Jesus. When people see us, they associate our activity with God's kingdom because we are ambassadors of reconciliation. Our whole job is to invite them into the presence of God, into the presence they were always meant to carry.

The God whose image we bear is the God who never gives up. And his reputation is at stake in our lifestyle. How we live reflects on who he is.

This is the moment when we want to say, "I can't do that! That responsibility is too enormous."

You're Not Alone

It sounds like a big task. Just sharing the gospel with others sounds scary enough—but now we're meant to live entire lives that witness to and work toward reconciliation? If that sounds overwhelming, you're not alone.

So it's a good thing we don't do this work alone. It's a responsibility we carry together.

We're all ambassadors together. At Pentecost the Spirit was poured out on a large group of disciples. The early church was unified in heart and soul. It takes a whole community to convey the culture of the kingdom of God.

Our life together in Christ is an outpost of the kingdom, a pocket of the new creation. We can't be an outpost of the kingdom as individuals. One Chinese restaurant alone doesn't make Chinatown. A whole community of people from the same country creates an outpost where visitors can feel like they've stepped into another place. It's a place where everything looks, smells, sounds, tastes, and feels different. But in our case it's the sights and sounds of God's kingdom.

This is why we need to be sure the kingdom we're reflecting together is the kingdom of God—the overlapping of heaven and earth—and not the reign of death. We need to know God as both our Father and our King, the one who is glad to be with us and who is trusting us with the blessing of the family business. We need to reflect God with us and God through us. When we see one another as brothers and sisters in the same family and ambassadors of the same King, we can "spur one another on toward" connection with God and contribution to the family mission (Hebrews 10:24 NIV).

Heaven's Resources

Not only do we have God's presence in the Holy Spirit, but we also have all the resources of the kingdom of God. By the presence of the Holy Spirit with us and in us, Jesus gives us all the power and authority that was given to him to do the things that he did.

In the Gospel of Luke we saw Jesus working powerfully in the Spirit. Reading the book of Acts, we find the early church bearing the same power and authority through the Spirit. We see people who are at odds with God brought into God's family. We see the sick healed, demons cast out, the lame walk, the blind see, the dead brought back to life. This is heaven coming down to earth. This is the longed-for overlapping of heaven and earth.

This is the culture of the kingdom of God. This is the foretaste of what is to come! This is the ministry of reconciliation at its best. This is the business we contribute to as children and ambassadors connected to our Father and King. This is where we belong, and this is how we become a blessing to the whole world. This is the "joy set before him" that Jesus longed for when he carried the cross to his death and was raised back to life.

Practice: Immanuel Journaling

- Begin with gratitude. What things—both big and small—can you thank God for today? How does he respond to your gratitude? What might he say to you about that?
- What does God see when he looks at you today? Let him speak in the first person: "I see you sitting in your favorite chair, wearing . . ."
- What does God hear when he listens to your thoughts? "I hear you wondering about . . . worrying about . . . excited about . . . frustrated about . . ."
- What does it feel like to remember that God meets you where you are, seeing you and hearing your thoughts and feelings?

- What does God understand about what he's seeing and hearing? "I understand how big this is . . . I know how long you've been waiting . . . I understand how you got here . . . I get it. I know."
- Let God express his joy in being with you, right here and right now where you really are. "I'm glad to be with you in this."
- How might God be *for* you in this? How might he want to flourish your life and bless the people in your life? "I'm doing something here . . . I'm making all things new . . . I'm flourishing your life by . . ."[1]

Reflection

Think about the way you generally live and treat people. What kind of impression might people get about the kingdom of God from knowing you?

Talk to God about your capacity to be an ambassador of reconciliation, and seek reconciliation with him about this.

Song

As you listen to "Build Your Kingdom Here" by Rend Collective, in what ways do you long for God's kingdom to come in your family, neighborhood, workplace, or city?

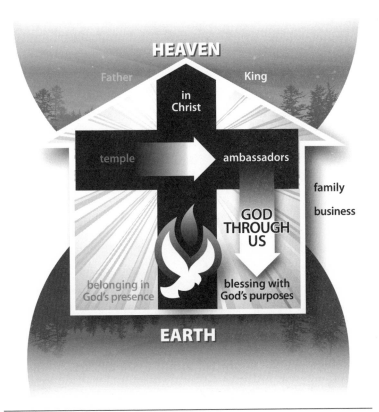

All people living in Christ—by the Spirit—are ambassadors of the King, extending the family business of blessing the world with God's purposes.

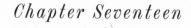

Chapter Seventeen

Can I Go Home Now?

*C*yd and I got married in 2000, just four months after Cyd's mom had died. For two months we continued to live in the coastal mountains of California where we had met. But since I was going to seminary in Chicago, we started getting ready to move.

We finished up at our jobs, said goodbye to friends, and visited favorite spots one last time. Things were messy, confusing, and unsettled. We were starting a major transition, and we were overwhelmed and discouraged.

To get through it we began to encourage each other with a hopeful mantra that always started with, "When we get to Chicago . . ."

- When we get to Chicago we'll figure out our budget.
- When we get to Chicago we'll learn how to communicate better.
- When we get to Chicago life will settle down.
- When we get to Chicago things will return to normal.
- When we get to Chicago . . .

Finally, we packed all of our belongings into our '87 Subaru hatchback and headed across the country. We visited Sequoia National Park and the Grand Canyon. We spent time with friends in Arizona and New Mexico. We dodged a tornado in Kansas.

And all along the way, when difficult or confusing things came up, we would tell each other, "Let's work that out when we get to Chicago."

Finally, we were in our new apartment in Chicago. But things didn't settle down. Life didn't become normal. Everything was not easier all of a sudden.

We needed to set up utilities: gas, electricity, a phone line. We needed to find the grocery store, find a new church, and figure out a zillion other little things. On top of all that, Cyd needed to find a job. And I was about to start a summer-long intensive class to learn Greek.

So instead of *When we get to Chicago . . .* we starting thinking *When Cyd gets a job . . .* and *When Geoff finishes with Greek.* And then it was, *When Cyd finds a better job . . .* and *When Geoff finishes the first semester . . .* And on and on it went. We kept moving the finish line for when life would become normal, when things would be easy and make sense.

Eventually, it became a joke between us. After living for more than a year in Chicago, whenever something difficult would happen we would just throw up our hands and say, "When we get to Chicago . . ." Now that we're settling into life in Grand Rapids, we still say, "When we get to Chicago . . ." to lighten the situation.

Longing for Home

Don't we all do this?

We mark our lives by these events and transitions, things a little bit ahead of us, when life will really start, when some problem will end, when some stressor will be behind us, and we can relax again. We can get back to "normal" again.

Maybe it's when you finish high school or graduate from college. Or when you have a better friend or a special someone. Or the perfect job or a bigger paycheck. When you lose the weight, when the kids move out, after surgery, and so on.

We end up placing our hope in these events and transitions—these self-imposed mile markers. In the meantime we live overwhelmed and disoriented lives because we're always waiting for the next thing that will make everything else fall into place. And what is it that we really desire?

We all long for a place to call home, a place to belong, a place from which to bless. As we bounce around from house to house, job to job, and city to city, as we weave between romantic relationships and stressful friendships, as we aim to change the world and make a difference, ultimately we long for a place where we belong and an opportunity to bless others.

Our hope in life is to have meaningful connections and to make lasting contributions in the world. Our hope is to have deep relationships and a wide impact. But after a life of disappointments and heartbreaks we shrink these desires to as small as possible and lay out little mile markers for a life that is headed who knows where.

What are you placing your hope in? Where is your hope leading you? The desires for meaningful connections and lasting contributions are good. These are the desires to belong and to be a blessing. But it matters where you place your hope for these.

Ultimately, our desires to belong and to be a blessing are fulfilled at the last mile marker in our journey of God with us. This last mile marker is the full union of heaven and earth when Jesus comes again. What Jesus has started in the past and what followers of Jesus experience partially in the present, we will enjoy fully in the future.

One day, Jesus will return and unite heaven and earth in an unimaginable way.

But too often we can feel like the return of Jesus is a catchphrase or wishful thinking, like when Cyd and I turned "When we get to Chicago . . ." into a joke.

The Promised Ending

We often focus on the wrong things when we think about the coming of Jesus. When will he come? What are the signs? What must we do to speed his approach? Much time and ink have been spent deciphering the book of Revelation in order to prepare for Jesus' second coming.

We need to shift our focus from trying to figure out when it will all end to remembering what the promised end is. The end of Revelation speaks of God's presence and purposes being fulfilled in the union of heaven and earth. It speaks of our belonging and blessing with and through God. It speaks of God's home becoming our home.

Revelation 21 opens with John seeing a new heaven and a new earth, and the new Jerusalem—the perfect city—coming down from God. And a voice from God's throne declares the meaning of all this, saying,

> See, the *home of God* is among mortals.
> He will *dwell with them*;
> they will be his peoples,
> and God himself will be with them. (Revelation 21:3,
>   emphasis added)

Twice we are reminded that God will be with his people in the end. Why is God with his people? Because God's home—God's dwelling place—is with humanity once again. No longer are the heavens and the earth separated. No longer is God's home separated from our home. We will forever belong in God' presence.

And what are the benefits of belonging with God? We are told that

> He will wipe every tear from their eyes.
> Death will be no more;
> mourning and crying and pain will be no more,
> for the first things have passed away. (Revelation 21:4)

All tears of shame and disappointment, all tears of sorrow and regret, all the tears of abuse and hate will be wiped away by the hand of God. When our home is with God, our most intimate longings will be fulfilled. The reign of death will be destroyed in our lives, our relationships, our hearts.

The life that Jesus began when he planted life inside the reign of death will now flourish unhindered. The battle will finally be over. All the powers and forces of evil will cease their fighting. Sin, shame, and death will be broken. We will no longer wonder whether God really likes us. We will know beyond any doubt that God is our Father who delights in us and constantly calls us his beloved. We will never wonder if God is a good King or if he wants us around or if he trusts us. We will know our place of belonging, and we will be a blessing. The gates will be thrown open and the nations will stream into the city of God. The tree of life will be in the center of the city, and its leaves will bring healing and hope to all the nations.

But this can sound so far off and mystical. Are we just going to wander around in a perfect city giving each other high fives as we go? Isn't heaven going to be a little boring? Sure, it'll be great that the reign of death is overcome, but that seems so abstract. Does it go any deeper than this?

Face to Face

Yes, it does. In the union of heaven and earth, we will see God face-to-face (Revelation 22:4).

When it comes to faces, I (Geoff) feel I have a pretty forgettable face. Well into my thirties I assumed that people would not remember or recognize me. I would often reintroduce myself to people just to have them say, "Yeah, I remember you," in a semi-offended kind of way.

I was convinced that if I put on a baseball cap I would become utterly unrecognizable. Like Superman slipping on eyeglasses and suddenly becoming Clark Kent, I had this weird idea that with a hat on, I would become invisible.

I know this sounds ridiculous. But you need to know I have an identical twin brother. Growing up, people really didn't know who I was. People knew I was one of the Holsclaw Twins, but they weren't sure which one. At school, playing sports, at church—I was just

Holsclaw. People, even good friends, would rather call me by my last name than mess up my first name.

It wasn't until later in life that I realized I was truly believing and acting as if I was forgettable, unmemorable, unknown.

A particular memory I have illustrates this. I was nineteen or twenty and visiting home from college. I went out to breakfast with my dad. While the conversation was pleasant, a cloud began growing in my mind. I hadn't seen my dad in a while, and as we were talking—really, just chitchatting about this or that—I noticed he wasn't asking questions about me, about what I was up to or working toward. We were just talking about neutral topics. I had a growing feeling that my dad didn't know what I was interested in or what my hopes were. He didn't know what I longed for or was afraid of. He didn't know what to ask to draw me out.

And then all at once it hit me. My own dad didn't know me. I was his son! But he was talking to me like I was just a casual acquaintance. He wasn't talking to me like he really knew me.

I was probably too young to realize just how much that experience hurt—and how it confirmed the message that I was unseen and unknown. I probably just decided that my dad was a little too set in his ways, doing the best he could. Or to be honest, I was pretty emotionally disconnected at age twenty, and I'm sure I just ignored the pain as quickly as I had realized it.

I longed to be known face-to-face, in person. We all do.

To Be Known and Loved

In the final union of heaven and earth, only love will remain, for love never fails (1 Corinthians 13:8 NIV). The apostle Paul says this, "For now we see in a mirror, dimly, but then we will see face to face. Now I know only in part; then I will know fully, *even as I have been fully known*" (1 Corinthians 13:12, emphasis added). To be loved and fully known is to experience a love in which there is no fear (1 John 4:18).

In their sin Adam and Eve feared God and lived in shame. They hid from God. Just like them, we hide in fear and live in shame. How much of our fear of God is really just fear of having our shame exposed? Or maybe it is fear that no one really knows and understands us. Or worst of all, fear that someone does know and understand us and cannot be trusted with this knowledge.

But God knows everything about us and continues to pursue us just as he pursued Adam and Eve in the Garden. He pursues us not because he has to but because he wants to. God already knows us and still loves us. We hide our faces from God in shame even though it is only in relationship with God—the only one who sees us completely and still loves us entirely—that our shame can be removed.

Why does being known by God overcome our shame? Because when all of our filth is exposed and someone is still glad to be with us, the disconnection disappears. Only joy remains. Only love remains. God is always glad to be with us because he knows not just who we are but who we will become—who we were always meant to be. He knows that we *belong* in his presence and that we can *bless* others with his purposes. He knows we are extremely important to him and to the future of the world.

Being known by God is a reason for peace, not fear. It's cause for joy, not shame. Being known by God is to be loved. And it means that God, indeed, likes you. He doesn't only love you because he has to. He doesn't just put up with you or tolerate you because he promised he would. He actually wants to be with you. He's always wanted to be with you. He delights in you as someone who uniquely images him and his longing for the world. He saved you for this joy.

And this is what we long for: to be known. We want to be able to look into the face of God, to experience his gaze as the gaze of love, and to be transformed by that love. To be known and loved, face-to-face, is to return home and to return to joy.

The City Museum

This transformation by love is on full display at the City Museum in St. Louis, Missouri. The name makes it sound like a place to learn about the history of St. Louis, which sounded a little boring to us. But good friends kept telling us we should check it out.

It was not at all what we expected. The entire museum is literally made of junk—the junk of the city transformed into a playground wonderland. The whole museum is composed of pieces of St. Louis that had been demolished, abandoned, or thrown away as useless. Concrete, rebar, rusty gears, cinder blocks, ceiling panels, broken tiles, shards of pottery, empty beer kegs, broken bottles—all things that had been tossed aside as worthless or unusable. To use the language of this book, everything was tossed aside because it didn't belong anymore.

But the builders of the City Museum didn't see it that way. They transformed this trash into a beautiful, eclectic playground for children and adults. One room transforms scraps into a swampland forest people can swing through. Another room is a maze of bank safes and mirrors. Another is full of ladders and slides—one slide is ten stories tall! Outside people can climb high into the air through "gerbil tunnels" made of rebar, into a broken airplane suspended in the air, or onto a dilapidated school bus hanging off the side of the building. As a family we have spent hours—actually days—exploring the different rooms, finding secret passageways, and delighting in unexpected treasures. And the whole thing is not only fun to play in, but it's also surprisingly beautiful. The whole place is a work of art.

Without vision and purpose, these cast-off and abandoned construction materials had no value. But an artist saw them, pieced them together, and gave them a home, and a new and marvelous playground was born—a place full of joy. A place where people can play like children and experience delight. A place that blesses hundreds of people every day.

The City Museum is a picture of how we are known by God. Even when we feel like trash, God knows what we can become—an amazing new creation transformed in love. And this new creation is the home we've all been longing for.

Practice: Imagining New Creation

When God sees you, he not only sees you as you are but also how you are becoming exactly who he designed you to be. Take some time to be honest about the things in your life that seem wasted or purposeless and ask God how you might offer these parts to him to be repurposed to become places of joy and blessing to others.

Reflection

Have you ever been apart from someone you love for a period of time? What was it like to communicate by phone, email, text, even FaceTime?

In what ways did you find yourself longing to be with them in person again?

What do you think it will be like to finally see God face to face?

Song

As you listen to "Known" by Tauren Wells, think about how it would feel to be fully known and loved.

In Christ and by the Spirit, God's place of joy is restored to all things so that humanity can again live as God's beloved children and God's empowered ambassadors.

Acknowledgments

*W*e wouldn't be the people that we are without our seventeen years as a part of the kingdom outpost at Life on the Vine (Long Grove, IL). In that place we had the opportunity to shape and be shaped by kingdom culture and have a foretaste of the life to come. We are honored to be part of Vineyard North (Grand Rapids, MI) and are appreciative of the way you have thrown your arms open to us and welcomed us into the family, and we anticipate many years of flourishing together.

We are grateful for our friends at Gravity Leadership who have endeavored to make kingdom culture reproducible by offering concrete ways to live into abstract realities. We thank our brothers and sisters in the Ecclesia Network who continually make space for us, name and appreciate the ways they see Christ in us, and regularly encourage us to step further and deeper into the kingdom call on our lives. We are also deeply indebted to the work of Karl Lehman, Jim Wilder, and the broader Immanuel Prayer Movement, as catalysts for joy and healing in the companionship of Jesus through Immanuel Prayer and Journaling.

Last, we want to acknowledge all the fabulous people (especially Kathy, Marlene, and the folks at IVP) who were convinced that this good news needed to be written and were willing to support us on this journey.

Notes

Introduction

[1]N. T. Wright, *New Interpreter's Bible: Acts; Introduction to Epistolary Literature; Romans; 1 Corinthians*: 10 (Nashville: Abingdon, 2002), 384; Haley Goranson Jacob, *Conformed to the Image of His Son: Reconsidering Paul's Theology of Glory in Romans* (Downers Grove, IL: IVP Academic, 2018), 100-104.

[2]John Murray, *The Epistle to the Romans* (Grand Rapids: Eerdmans, 1980), 112-13.

1. What Is That Smell?

[1]E. James Wilder, Edward Kjouri, Christ Coursey, and Sheila D. Sutton, *Joy Starts Here* (East Peoria, IL: Shepherd's House, 2013), 7-9.

[2]Allan N. Schore, *Affect Regulation and the Repair of the Self* (New York: W. W. Norton, 2003), 37-45. Also see Daniel J. Siegel's seminal book, *The Developing Mind*, 2nd ed. (New York: Guilford Press, 2015), 162-77. E. James Wilder and Curt Thompson, among others, have integrated Schore's insights with a theological perspective. Wilder uses this integration throughout his works but most clearly explains the developmental longing of infants to seek the faces of and build their own identities in relation to their primary caregivers. See his *Living with Men* (Pasadena, CA: Shepherds House, 2004), 11-17. Curt Thompson, relying a bit more on Siegel, comes to the same conclusions in his integration of neuroscience and spiritual formation in *Anatomy of the Soul* (Carol Stream, IL: Tyndale House, 2010).

[3]Schore, *Affect Regulation*, 45; and Wilder, *Living with Men*, 16-21.

2. Where Is Home?

[1]For more on the Garden of Eden as a temple, see John H. Walton, *Lost World of Adam and Eve* (Downers Grove, IL: IVP Academic, 2009), 116-27; G. K. Beale, *The Temple and the Church's Mission: A Biblical Theology of the Dwelling Place of God* (Downers Grove, IL: IVP Academic, 2004), 66-80.

[2]Walton, *Lost World of Genesis One*, 86-91; Beale, *Temple and the Church*, 61.

3. Do I Belong Here?

[1]Biblical scholar and theologian N. T. Wright regularly refers to humanity as a mirror reflecting God's image into the world. See his *Surprised by Hope* (New York: HarperCollins, 2008), 94, 182, 207.

[2]This idea has its roots in 2 Corinthians 3:18 ("And all of us, with unveiled faces, seeing the glory of the Lord as though reflected in a mirror, are being transformed into the same image from one degree of glory to another"). We will return to this in part four.

[3]Catherine McDowell, *The Image of God in the Garden of Eden* (University Park, PA: Eisenbrauns, 2015), 118.

[4]McDowell, *Image of God*, 117-77.

[5]Daniel J. Siegel, *The Developing Mind*, 2nd ed. (New York: Guilford Press, 2015), 164-71.

5. Does God Really Like Me?

[1]Brené Brown, "Shame vs. Guilt," *Brené Brown* (blog), January 14, 2013, https://brenebrown.com/blog/2013/01/14/shame-v-guilt/.

[2]Curt Thompson, *The Soul of Shame* (Downers Grove, IL: InterVarsity Press, 2015), 99.

[3]Thompson, *Soul of Shame*, 100-107. See also Thompson's expanded commentary on the fall in his *Anatomy of the Soul* (Carol Stream, IL: Tyndale House, 2010), 207-20.

6. Why Do I Have to Wait?

[1]In the book of Genesis Abraham is first called Abram, and Sarah is at first called Sarai. They are later renamed by God in Genesis 17. But to avoid confusion we will just always call them Abraham and Sarah.

[2]We explained this name change in note 1.

[3]The practice of Immanuel journaling is described in E. James Wilder, Anna Kang, and John Loppnow, *Joyful Journey: Listening to Immanuel* (East Peoria, IL: Shepherd's House, 2015).

7. Is God Angry with Me?

[1]The practice of Immanuel journaling is described in E. James Wilder, Anna Kang, and John Loppnow, *Joyful Journey: Listening to Immanuel* (East Peoria, IL: Shepherd's House, 2015).

8. Is God Disappointed with Me?

[1]Shankar Vedantam, "Lost in Translation," *Hidden Brain*, NPR, January 29, 2018, www.npr.org/templates/transcript/transcript.php?storyId=581657754.

9. Is God Done with Me?

[1]Crispin Fletcher-Louis, "God's Image, His Cosmic Temple and the High Priest," in *Heaven on Earth: The Temple in Biblical Theology*, ed. Simon Gathercole (Waynesboro, GA: Paternoster, 2004), 81-99.

[2]Shankar Vedantam, "How President Trump's Rhetoric Is Changing the Way Americans Talk," *Hidden Brain*, *NPR*, September 4, 2017, www.npr .org/templates/transcript/transcript.php?storyId=548471325.

16. Did I Really Sign Up for This?

[1]The practice of Immanuel journaling is described in E. James Wilder, Anna Kang, and John Loppnow, *Joyful Journey: Listening to Immanuel* (East Peoria, IL: Shepherd's House, 2015).